CW00506772

Poems From The South
Edited by Donna Samworth

 Young**Writers**

First published in Great Britain in 2008 by:
Young Writers
Remus House
Coltsfoot Drive
Peterborough
PE2 9JX
Telephone: 01733 890066
Website: www.youngwriters.co.uk

All Rights Reserved

© Copyright Contributors 2008

SB ISBN 978-1 84431 611 3

Foreword

Young Writers was established in 1991 and has been passionately devoted to the promotion of reading and writing in children and young adults ever since. The quest continues today. Young Writers remains as committed to the nurturing of poetic and literary talent as ever.

This year's Young Writers competition has proven as vibrant and dynamic as ever and we are delighted to present a showcase of the best poetry from across the UK and in some cases overseas. Each poem has been selected from a wealth of *Little Laureates 2008* entries before ultimately being published in this, our seventeenth primary school poetry series.

Once again, we have been supremely impressed by the overall quality of the entries we have received. The imagination, energy and creativity which has gone into each young writer's entry made choosing the poems a challenging and often difficult but ultimately hugely rewarding task - the general high standard of the work submitted ensured this opportunity to bring their poetry to a larger appreciative audience.

We sincerely hope you are pleased with this final collection and that you will enjoy *Little Laureates 2008 Poems From The South* for many years to come.

Contents

Bentley Primary School, Farnham

Chloe Drewitt (10)   50
Loni Stephens (9)   50
Reid Brown (10)   51
Joshua Young (9)   51
Henry Penman (9)   52
Katie Lewis (10)   52
Nicole Carslake (9)   53
Callum Wilkins (9)   53
Sophie Guyon (10)   54

Pensans Commuity Primary School, Penzance
Solomon Davis (10)   54
Morgan Jones (9)   55
Madeleine Ead (10)   55
Cloe Carter (9)   56
Tamsin Weeks (9)   56

Priory RC Primary School, Torquay
Jake Price (10)   56
Luchia Valenti (10)   57
Nicholas Stott (10)   57
Jade Harris (10)   58
Adelina Schiano (10)   58
Olivia Bickley (10)   59
Jordan Leleivre (11)   59
Lucy Jane Meacock (10)   60
Danielle Lee (11)   60
William Nicolle (10)   61

St David's School, Purley
James Nash (11)   61
Natasha Phillips (10)   62
Emily Jones (11)   62

St John's Meads CE Primary School, Eastbourne
Miles Edwards (11)   63
Tom Roberts (7)   63
Max Marshall (7)   64
Sasha Vieira (7)   64
Phoebe Hepburn (7)   64

Louis Wilson (7)	65
Maddy Smith (7)	65
Sophie Lucas (8)	65
Stan Garbett (8)	66
Mary Oakenfold (8)	66

St John's Primary School, Woking

Jordan Appleyard (11)	67
Abbey Palmer (11)	67
Ryan Cree (11)	68
Bethany Westwood (10)	68
Lacey Meredith (10)	69

St Thomas Garnet's School, Bournemouth

Claire Martin (9)	69
Nicholas Beaumont (10)	70
Jeremy Sobisch (9)	70
Matthew Giddens (10)	71
Gabriella St Clair-Hefler (9)	71
Piers Verstage (9)	72
Frankie Skinner (11)	72
Dominic Hughes (10)	73
Matthew Thomson (11)	73
Jean-Jacques Coppini (11)	74
Rebecca Giddens (10)	74
Diarmid Becker (11)	75
Georgia MacDonald-Taylor (9)	75
Kira Allum (8)	76
Joshua Allum (10)	76
Rosheen Daly (8)	76
Katherine Brereton (11)	77
Nikan Houshmand-Motlagh (7)	77
Scott Austin (8)	77
Joseph Yeadon (9)	78
Eva Becker (8)	78
Eleanor Austin (11)	79
Lucy Taylor (7)	79
Gina Davis (7)	79
Lily Newton (8)	80
Sophie Sawyer (8)	80

Sandcross School, Reigate

Eleanor Riches (9)	81
Harriet Wood (9)	81
Daisy Moon (10)	82
Georgie Coram (10)	82

Sheet Primary School, Petersfield

Eleanor Burford (9)	83

Sherwell Valley Primary School, Torquay

William Price (7)	83
Martha Downs (8)	84
Amy Potter (7)	84
Angel Harper (7)	85
Izzy Huddart (8)	85
Amelia Simpson (7)	86
Tierney Leaver (7)	86
Laurie Ahearne (7)	86
James Campbell (8)	87
Louis Egan (8)	87
Adam Smith (8)	87
Lloyd Higgins (7)	88
Kieran Moore (7)	88
Sam Davies (8)	88
Lizzie Rodda (7)	89
Max Robinson (8)	89
Naomi Wilson (8)	89
Freya Woods (7)	90
Felix Nicholls (8)	90
Bethany England (7)	90
Ame Toms	91
Millie Wigington (8)	91
Nandaja Narayanan (8)	91
Chloe Ratcliffe (7)	92
Rebecca Roots (8)	92
Maisie Tysall (7)	93
Haydon Green (8)	93
Owen Dawe-Smith (8)	93
Lily James (8)	94
Jazmin Sherlock (8)	94
Indie-May Taylor (8)	94

Kai Draper (8)	95
Molly Hughes (8)	95
Maxwell Pike (8)	95
Ryan Owen (7)	96
Jess Goss (7)	96
Eloise Jackson (8)	96
Jacob Hogan (8)	97
Chase Ahearne (7)	97
Rachel Jones & Leah Gardner (8)	97
Megan King (7)	98
Ryan Storey-Day (7), Harry Jamieson & Luke Lewis (8)	98

Stuart Road Primary School, Plymouth

Miella Hayles (8)	99
Tia Woolcock (9)	100
James Braidford (8)	101
Jake Donkin-Peters (9)	102
Tara Waterfield (8)	102

The Clinton CE Primary School, Merton

Abby Fletcher (9)	103
Chelsey Weeks (9)	103
Annabel Halstead (9)	103
Charlotte Swain (9)	104
Chris Ashton (10)	104
Danielle Payne (10)	105
Hannah Loufer (11)	105
Pip Mahoney (9)	106
Thomas Wright (9)	106
Emily Hookway (10)	107
Lydia Wade (10)	107
Megan Chapman (9)	108
Aidan Wright (8)	108
Lauren Butler (11)	109

Thorner's CE Primary School, Dorchester

Greg Bolam-Green (10)	109
Annie Nobes (9)	109
Aaron Sinclair (10)	110
Imogen Slade (9)	110
Flora Jevons (10)	111

Vinehall School, Robertsbridge

Woolacombe School, Woolacombe

The Poems

The Poem

I Will Capture In My Box

(Inspired by 'Magic Box' by Kit Wright)

I will capture in my box . . .
The slither of a snake on a silent night
The golden gleam of a goldfish
Having a ride on Tony Hawks' skateboard.

I will capture in my box . . .
The first words of a brand new teddy
Shaking the hand of Mickey Mouse
The sun smiling down on all of the planets.

I will capture in my box . . .
The roar of a crowd for the winning wrestling champion
My first bike ride without falling off
The last Smartie in the packet.

I will capture in my box . . .
A giraffe with long black and white stripes
A yellow zebra with brown spots
A black sun and an orange Earth.

Darcy Dawson-Siggs (10)
Bentley Primary School, Farnham

In My Dream

In my dream I saw
A cute, black, baby, chubby chimp crawling slowly towards me.

In my dream I heard
A big black mountain gorilla beating his enormous drum tummy.

In my dream I brushed
The hairy tummy of an orang-utan, it felt like a soft fluffy carpet.

In my dream I tasted
A juicy mango fruit sloshing around in my mouth.

In my dream I screamed,
'Oh, argh, oh, argh!'

Alexander Toft (10)
Bentley Primary School, Farnham

In My Dream

In my dream I saw . . .
A humungous, fluffy, black cat
Catch a tiny, black, fluffy mouse.

In my dream I heard . . .
The bright bluebirds twittering together
Like a huge meeting on the fizzy electric wire.

In my dream I felt . . .
The long thin grass brush against my face
Like a bristly carpet.

In my dream I could taste . . .
The ruby-red, ripe, juicy English apples
On the multicoloured dancing trees.

In my dream I said . . .
To the black cat,
'Did you know that the sun
Is a humungous ball of flaming gas?'

Celeste Wickins (10)
Bentley Primary School, Farnham

In My Dream

In my dream I saw a slick silver stallion
Swaying his mane in the frozen wind.

In my dream I heard the hiss, hiss of a petrifying python
Slithering silently through the matted undergrowth.

In my dream I felt rough ragged skin
Like the hard scratchy bark on the colossal shadowing trees.

In my dream I could taste the bitter freezing icy taste
Of the dirty, cloudy, polluted air around me.

In my dream I said,
'The moon is a cat's eye staring at me
Waking me from a deep sleep.'

Billie Price (9)
Bentley Primary School, Farnham

In My Dream

In my dream I saw
A glittering sea horse like the strong sea
Rushing, smashing and crashing against the solid rocks.

In my dream I heard
An enormous howl horridly like the clap of thunder.

In my dream I felt a dog's paw scratch my cheek
And his fur against my soft skin as he touched me.

In my dream I could taste smoked salmon
Freshly cooked, fall smoothly down out of my mouth
As its warmth touched my soft insides.

In my dream I screamed,
'The sun is a huge red ball of burning petrol.'

Adam Murphy (10)
Bentley Primary School, Farnham

In My Dream . . .

In my dream I saw a great, big, titanic temple
Rise from behind the hovering hills.

In my dream I heard a beggar boy cry out to the dancing crows
As the blasting bomb went off - *bang!*

In my dream I felt the cold wind clasp my fingers
Like my mama's shivering hands.

In my dream I could taste the baking batches
Of soft, crumbly, chocolate cake next door.

In my dream I whispered,
'The moon is a dancing, sparkling, silver ball
Gazing over the spectacular sea!'

Lucy Siers (10)
Bentley Primary School, Farnham

My Magic Box
(Based on 'Magic Box' by Kit Wright)

I will keep in my box . . .
A flash of a cheetah sprinting after its prey
A bonfire flickering flames in the corner of a garden
A silly monkey messing around with money.

I will keep in my box . . .
The sun facing down on the world like a brother
Looking down on his little sister
The headlight on a car like a dog's eyes glowing in the darkness.

I will keep in my box . . .
The first tooth from my baby sister Amelia
The kick of my first football
The last mouthful of my double chocolate milkshake.

I will keep in my box . . .
My dog walking on its lead
The thirteenth month with the bluest moon
Giraffes with grey bodies
And an elephant with brown spots.

Alicia Cooper (9)
Bentley Primary School, Farnham

In My Dream

In my dream
I saw a frog flip dramatically on to a lily pad
In my dream I heard a dung beetle tip-tap across a path
In my dream I felt an ant tickle me as he scuttled rapidly over my hand
In my dream I tasted the horrible taste of water sliding into my mouth
Like a snail sliding over my arm
In my dream I asked, 'Is this really happening to me?'

Gabriel Hawkes (9)
Bentley Primary School, Farnham

I'm The Target

Help! Help! Help!
Why do people bully?
It makes you feel small
And very, very lonely
They pull my hair
Then they laugh
It's so unfair
I need some help
The tease me all the time
Bullying is such a terrible crime
I'm bruised
I'm hurt
They even ripped my best white shirt.
I'm 'four eyes'
I'm 'zip mouth'
I'm different they say.
Oh why don't they stop bullying?
Oh why, oh why, oh why?
They should stop some day
Or someone's going to find out.

Yasmin Bedwell-Garcia (10)
Bentley Primary School, Farnham

In My Dream . . .

In my dream I saw a crouched crow crawl onto the cluttered
church roof
In my dream I heard the announcing whisper of the cranky trees
As if they were going to crumble to their knobbly knees
In my dream I felt the coldness like icy claws from an ice lion digging
deeper and deeper
In my dream I could taste a splash of honey in my hungry mouth
With the never-ending sweetness
In my dream I said, 'This is the most unreal world I've been to.'

Charlotte Nutt (9)
Bentley Primary School, Farnham

In My Dream

In my dream I saw a dark horse as black as burnt coal
Crunching through the misty forest, breathing deep long breaths.
The cold icy wind, blowing its shadowy face
Its eyes like long dark tunnels
Sweeping the leafy earth, its hair like long thin snakes
Curling around its skinny neck
Its long legs like willow saplings.

In my dream I heard the green thin leaves on the tall bony trees
Rustle in the strong, icy, cold wind
The trunks of the saplings bending over so much
They looked like they were going to snap
The wind was like a cold breath blowing the leaves of the snowy trees.

In my dream I felt as hot as the fiery sun on a summer's day
The sweat was running down my face as I galloped through the trees
My cloven hooves ached, my antlers as spiky as sharp knives
My eyes watered and my nose ran
I was scared stiff. My heart pounded like a hammer!

Daisy Clarke (9)
Bentley Primary School, Farnham

Worrying Target

I felt bruised and tormented
I was small, cornered and hurt
They were laughing, hitting and teasing me
I'm helpless and terrified
I wept all alone
It was unfair and cruel
I felt puzzled and vulnerable
I am different
I am angry
It is so unfair.

Charlotte Desmond (9)
Bentley Primary School, Farnham

In My Dream

In my dream I saw a golden spotty cheetah
Sprinting after a light brown deer
Like an Olympic runner trying to win a race.

In my dream I heard the clear blue rain
Pouring down like a cute skinny baby crying for its mum.

In my dream I felt the cold icy snowflakes
Land on my arm and dribble down the car window.

In my dream I tasted the creamy chocolate ice cream
Run down my pink smooth throat
Like someone tickling my mouth with a feather.

In my dream I said,
'Hiss, hiss,' like a snake crawling up a knobbly trunk of a tree.

Cicely Hayes (9)
Bentley Primary School, Farnham

In My Dream

In my dream I saw a slimy sly slug
Slopping along the green grass hissing to the colossal tree.

In my dream I heard a *crash, bang*
Of silver pots walloping onto the dusty dirty floor.

In my dream I felt a smooth soft snake
Like a million eyeballs all stuck together.

In my dream I could taste a sweet sugary taste of sherbet lemon
My whole mouth felt like it was going to explode.

In my dream I said, 'The moon is a ball of light
Shimmering over the silent world like a disco ball.'

Matilda White (9)
Bentley Primary School, Farnham

My Magic Box

(Based on 'Magic Box' by Kit Wright)

I will place in my box . . .
The flash of a fish leaping out of the crystal water
A delicate dolphin diving into the waves.

I will place in my box . . .
The moon smiling down on the Earth
Like a mother smiling at her beautiful baby
The headlights of a car like a cat's eyes glowing in the darkness.

I will place in my box . . .
The last glimpse of the angelfish disappearing into the coral
And the joy of my first pony ride.

I will place in my box . . .
The eighth day of the week
And the thirteenth month of the year.

My box is fashioned in pure gold
Lined with royal red velvet
The hinges are made from dolphin fins.

I will scuba-dive in my box in the bluest sea in Greece
And ride in the Olympics on the blackest horse for the England team.

Scarlet Mayes (9)
Bentley Primary School, Farnham

In My Dream Poem . . .

In my dream I saw the sun melting rapidly
Like Dairy Milk chocolate in an oven.

In my dream I heard the crash of thunder
Echoing in the night sky.

In my dream I felt the icy-cold snowdrop
Fall delicately onto my body.

In my dream I could taste the ocean in my mouth
As it dribbled down my throat.

In my dream I thought that my dream was alive.

George Barfoot (9)
Bentley Primary School, Farnham

My Magic Box

(Based on 'Magic Box' by Kit Wright)

I will keep in my box . . .
A scary shark swimming under the sunny sea
A perfect present from my baby brother
The colours of the rainbow in the clear sky.

I will keep in my box . . .
The setting sun behind the horizon
Casting shadows across the fields on a summer's night.

I will keep in my box . . .
My first win playing table tennis
My first goal in football
And my first school day in England.

I will keep in my box . . .
The eighth colour in the rainbow
The twenty-fifth hour of the day
And the second sun in the world.

My box is made from diamonds and gold stars
It is lined with dragon skin
I love my box.

Cyrus Wong (9)
Bentley Primary School, Farnham

In My Dream

In my dream I saw a galloping horse
As white as a crystal, glowing in the cold blue night.
Its eyes were shining in the starry darkness
Like a shimmering moon or a silver bowl floating in the spooky air.
The wind was blowing back its golden mane
It made everything shimmer as if it was magic.

In my dream I heard a high screech of a vicious hawk
It was like a racing Ferrari zooming all around the grounds
Making the wind blow through its fluffy feathers.

Ellis Bennett (10)
Bentley Primary School, Farnham

In My Magic Box

(Based on 'Magic Box' by Kit Wright)

I will keep in my box . . .
The sight of a swan splashing with its wings,
The first words of my baby brother, Tony,
The roar of the crowd as the winning goal crosses the line.

I will keep in my box . . .
A car with a frosty nose,
A sip of the coldest water on the hottest day,
A diamond sparkling in your eyes
And the flash of a cheetah zooming through the jungle.

I will keep in my box . . .
The last person on the planet,
The first smile of a baby,
A prayer spoken in Hindi and a blue moon.

I will keep in my box . . .
A person carrying an elephant,
The eighth day of the week
And the thirteenth month of the year.

My box is fashioned from gleaming diamonds
And lined with the mane of a lion
The lid is constructed from a rhino horn,
The hinges made from shark teeth.

I shall scuba-dive in my box in the great Atlantic Ocean,
And dive to the bottom of the sea to the wreck of the Armada.

Ollie Gowans (10)
Bentley Primary School, Farnham

The Magic Box

(Based on 'Magic Box' by Kit Wright)

I will place in my box . . .
A flicker of a flame glowing in the fire
The silence of a snake slithering in the sand
A green emerald glinting in the sun.

I will place in my box . . .
The headlights of a car glowing like my eyes looking back at me
My first special, deep-down secret
A fish leaping through the waves like a speedboat.

I will place in my box . . .
A first smile of a baby boy
The last sizzle of a sausage
The twinkle of a bright star shining in the sky.

I will place in my box . . .
The bright yellow gleam of the sun
A biker driving a Ferrari
A rally driver riding a Harley Davidson.

My box is constructed with dragon skin
With rubies and emeralds on the hinges
Its lid is made of silver segments, that glint like the moon
My box is protected by magic enchantments so nobody can touch it
but me.

I shall snowboard in my box in the Arctic
And have snow fights with snowmen
In the white fluffy snow, whenever I want.

James Kenyon (10)
Bentley Primary School, Farnham

Target

I was helpless
I did not know what to do
I was teased
I was laughed at
I was totally humiliated
I was also badly bruised
I was terrified.

I wept
It was very unfair
My best friend did not know what to do
It was just me
Why me?
Why me?
Why me?

I felt small
I tried to run but *no,* the bully pulled me back
A punch round the head . . .
I could not bear it
I was sad, as sad as an orphan all alone . . .
I was hurt
Bruised badly
Brutally the bully picked me up by the shirt and . . .
Threw me down on the floor
Ouch!

James Hearn (10)
Bentley Primary School, Farnham

The Writer Of This Poem

(Based on 'The Writer of this Poem' by Roger McGough)

The writer of this poem is taller than a tree
As bright as a bean
As pretty as a queen bee
As cheerful as a puppy
As shy as a mouse
As active as an athlete
As big as a house
As fun as a monkey
As funny as a bunny
As wiggly as a worm
As sweet as honey.

*'The writer of this poem never ceases to amaze
She's one in a million billion (or say the poem says)'!*

Gemma Williams (9)
Bentley Primary School, Farnham

Valentine Poem

My love for you burns a fiercely blazing fire
On a warm summer's evening
When I gaze into the black holes which are your eyes
I'm hypnotised and my heart would be heard thumping
More than a mile away.

Every hour, every minute, every second that you're not there
A part of me goes missing
A piece of the puzzle, not yet fitted.

Eden Day (11)
Bentley Primary School, Farnham

In My Dream

In my dream I saw . . .
A slimy toad go *plop* into the green weedy pond.

In my dream I heard . . .
The jolly chuckle of a colourful kookaburra in a flowering bush.

In my dream I felt . . .
The cold dusty iron bars on the end of my bed -
They felt like serpent snakes coiling around my hands.

In my dream I could taste . . .
The salty seawater with its white hands reaching forward onto the bay.

In my dream I said,
'Those stars are pearls, sparkling in the beautiful winter's night.'

Ella Kennett (9)
Bentley Primary School, Farnham

In My Dream

In my dream I saw the skeleton of the old, broken, fractured tree
Shining in the broken moonlight.

In my dream I heard the ear-splitting noise of a shell explode
In no-man's-land, sending sharp bits of shrapnel flying everywhere.

In my dream I felt the hard, metal-plated armour
Of the ferocious fighting tanks.

In my dream I tasted hot chunky chips
Which I but into and smelt a whiff of vinegar.

In my dream I shouted,
'All right lads . . . when the ramp goes down
I want you to run like Hell!'

Toby Remington (10)
Bentley Primary School, Farnham

The Writer Of This Poem

(Based on 'The Writer of this Poem' by Roger McGough)

The writer of this poem is smilier than everyone
As sweet as sugar
As fiery as a gun
As clever as a machine
As soft as a bunny
Eyes as bright as the stars
Hair as sleek and glossy as honey
A personality as kind as a bee's
A heart as big as a boulder
A brain as wise as an owl's
A person as useful as a folder.

*'The writer of this poem never ceases to amaze
She's one in a million billion (or so the poem says!)'*

Alicia Dent (9)
Bentley Primary School, Farnham

Valentine's Poem

I think of you in sunshine
I think of you in rain
I think of you when I'm happy
And also when I'm in pain.

You're my life, my love and my hero
I dream of you at night
Although you fill my phone with soppy texts
It makes me feel just right.

When I'm sad, you're there to cheer me up
I can count on you to care
My heart is yours forever
Never leave me, don't you dare!

Daisy Smith (10)
Bentley Primary School, Farnham

The Writer Of This Poem

(Based on 'The Writer of this Poem' by Roger McGough)

The writer of this poem is medium-sized like a bookshelf
As shy as a mouse
As light as a feather
As beautiful as a butterfly
As little as a pea
As scared as a cat
As smooth as a cushion can be
As keen as a mouse
As clean as a mountain
As shiny as an angel
As sunny as the sunshine.

*'The writer of this poem never ceases to amaze
She's one in a million billion (or so the poem says!)'*

Aveen Toma (9)
Bentley Primary School, Farnham

The Writer Of This Poem

(Based on 'The Writer of this Poem' by Roger McGough)

The writer of this poem is as bouncy as a clown
As blonde as a chicken
As busy as a town
As pretty as a poodle
As clever as a cow
As cute as a cat
As cool as that eyebrow
As naughty as a pony
As scared as a hedgehog
As intelligent as an elephant
As happy as a dog.

*'The writer of this poem never ceases to amaze
She's one in a million billion (or so the poem says!)'*

Rebecca Sutcliffe (9)
Bentley Primary School, Farnham

The Writer Of This Poem
(Based on 'The Writer of this Poem' by Roger McGough)

The writer of this poem has hair like bear's fur
Is as strong as an ox
As quiet as a cat's purr
As chunky as a box
As silky as a spider's web
As flat as a book
As wide as a bed
As creative as a cook
As happy as a busy bee
As angry as lightning
As fired up with joy and glee
As scary as someone frightening.

'The writer of this poem never ceases to amaze
He's one in a million billion (or so the poem says!)'

Maxwell Robinson (9)
Bentley Primary School, Farnham

The Writer Of This Poem
(Based on 'The Writer of this Poem' by Roger McGough)

The writer of this poem thinks deeper than the sea
Is redder than a volcano
Is sharper than a bee.

The writer of this poem is as talented as can be
Has a harder head than a rock
Funnier than a comedy.

The writer of this poem is stronger than a tree
Even more skilled than Robinho
And kinder than charity.

'The writer of this poem never ceases to amaze
He's one in a million billion (or so the poem says!)'

Guy Remington (8)
Bentley Primary School, Farnham

The Writer Of This Poem
(Based on 'The Writer of this Poem' by Roger McGough)

The writer of this poem is as silly as a monkey
As funny as someone gone crazy
And as cool as the sea
As flexible as a snake
As strong as a wrestler
As kind as a shake
As brown as a chocolate milk bar
As loud as a herd of elephants
As fast as a cheetah
As tall as a tree
As long as a metre.

'The writer of this poem never ceases to amaze
She's one in a million billion (or so the poem says!)'

Jasmine Payne (8)
Bentley Primary School, Farnham

The Writer Of This Poem
(Based on 'The Writer of this Poem' by Roger McGough)

The writer of this poem is as keen as can be
As friendly as a kitten
As clever as a bee
As happy as a bunny
As helpful as a teacher
As funny as a clown
As forgetful as a squirrel
As musical as a piano
As kind as an old tree
As playful as a puppy dog
As funky as a monkey.

'The writer of this poem never ceases to amaze
She's one in a million billion (or so the poem says!)'

Charlotte O'Connor (8)
Bentley Primary School, Farnham

The Writer Of This Poem

(Based on 'The Writer of this Poem' by Roger McGough)

The writer of this poem is taller than a door
As fast as a flash of wind
As thin as a piece of straw
She's just as chatty as a phone
And is very fun
As horsey as John Whittaker
Her hair as golden as the sun
As brave as a bear
As light as a feather
And loves looking at hares
As young as a lamb.

'The writer of this poem never ceases to amaze
She's one in a million billion (or so the poem says!)'

Eleanor Nightingale (9)
Bentley Primary School, Farnham

The Writer Of This Poem

(Based on 'The Writer of this Poem' by Roger McGough)

The writer of this poem is taller than a lamp post
As blonde as the sun
And does not like to boast
As sporty as a rugby player
As quick as a lightning bolt
As funny as a joke book
As strong as sour salt
As skinny as a pencil
As solid as a house
As skilled as a paper plane
As sneaky as a mouse.

'The writer of this poem never ceases to amaze
He's one in a million billion (or so the poem says!)'

Oscar Mosley (8)
Bentley Primary School, Farnham

The Writer Of This Poem

(Based on 'The Writer of this Poem' by Roger McGough)

The writer of this poem is as slim as a tree
As alert as an eagle
As busy as a bee
As netball crazy as Hannah Shake
As tennis mad as Maria Sharapova
As speedy as a Land Rover
As dozy as a dofus dog
As wise as a weasel
As bright as a buttercup
As singer crazy as Britney Spears
As cute as a pup.

'The writer of this poem never ceases to amaze
She's one in a million billion (or so the poem says!)'

Lydia Marks (8)
Bentley Primary School, Farnham

The Writer Of This Poem

(Based on 'The Writer of this Poem' by Roger McGough)

The writer of this poem is as friendly as a lamb
As magical as a magician
As pretty as a fan
˙As musical as a piano
As cool as a cow
As funky as a monkey
As soft as a miaow
As keen as a cat
As plain as a horse's mane
Hair as dark as a chocolate bar
As high as a plane.

'The writer of this poem never ceases to amaze
She's one in a million billion (or so the poem says!)/

Anna Hooker (9)
Bentley Primary School, Farnham

The Writer Of This Poem

(Based on 'The Writer of this Poem' by Roger McGough)

The writer of this poem is as bright as a tick
As quick as the wind
As smooth as a lick
Clean as new shoes
Eyes as blue as the sea
Hair as blonde as straw
And as shy as can be
As bubbly as a fish
As busy as a bee
As dainty as a swan
As helpful as a key.

*'The writer of this poem never ceases to amaze
She's one in a million billion (or so the poem says!)'*

Tatyana Dent (9)
Bentley Primary School, Farnham

The Writer Of This Poem

(Based on 'The Writer of this Poem' by Roger McGough)

The writer of this poem is as tall as a tree
As good as Man U
As kind as can be
As hard as a rock
As light as a key
As big as a train
And giggles with glee
As fun as a monkey
As brave as a bear
As strong as a rhino
And full with care.

*'The writer of this poem never ceases to amaze
He's one in a million billion (or so the poem says!)'*

Arran Deere (9)
Bentley Primary School, Farnham

The Writer Of This Poem

(Based on 'The Writer of this Poem' by Roger McGough)

The writer of this poem is as weak as a pea
As light as a feather
As crazy as a monkey
As clever as an elephant
As chatty as a chatterbox
As giggly as a hyena
As cunning as a fox
As tricky as a fib
As funny as a clown
As flexible as a snake
As busy as a town.

*'The writer of this poem never ceases to amaze
She's one in a million billion (or so the poem says!)'*

Jessica Cray (8)
Bentley Primary School, Farnham

The Writer Of This Poem

(Based on 'The Writer of this Poem' by Roger McGough)

The writer of this poem is taller than a tree
As clever as the eggheads
As hard as a knee
As bold as a boxing glove
A jumper as green as a tree
As good as a puppy
As handsome as can be
As blond as a yellow pencil
As busy as a bee
Is such a Man U supporter
And he loves a cup of tea.

*'The writer of this poem never ceases to amaze
He's one in a million billion (or so the poem says!)'*

Jamie Cradock (8)
Bentley Primary School, Farnham

The Writer Of This Poem

(Based on 'The Writer of this Poem' by Roger McGough)

The writer of this poem is as tall as a tree
As crazy as a moonling
As sharp as a bee
As light as a feather
As thin as a stick
As brave as a bear
As quick as a flick
As mighty as a boxer
As pointed as a nib
As golden as the sunshine
As tricky as a fib.

*'The writer of this poem never ceases to amaze
He's one in a million billion (or so the poem says!)'*

Matthew Cox (9)
Bentley Primary School, Farnham

The Writer Of This Poem

(Based on 'The Writer of this Poem' by Roger McGough)

The writer of this poem doesn't live in a town
Is as tall as a bookcase
And can turn upside-down
Has hair as flat as paper
As small as a fly
As fast as lightning
As sneaky as a lie
Mouth as big as a mountain
As sporty as a rugby player
As thin as a pencil
As clever as a mayor.

*'The writer of this poem never ceases to amaze
He's one in a million billion (or so the poem says!)'*

Jonathan Becker Davies (9)
Bentley Primary School, Farnham

The Writer Of This Poem

(Based on 'The Writer of this Poem' by Roger McGough)

The writer of this poem is as small as can be
As light as a feather
As friendly as a bee
As silly as a clown
As bouncy as a kangaroo
As giggly as a hyena
Hair as shiny as a new horseshoe
As weak as a leek
As funny as a chimpanzee
As cheeky as a monkey
As busy as a bee.

'The writer of this poem never ceases to amaze
She's one in a million billion (or so the poem says!)'

Phoebe Cray (8)
Bentley Primary School, Farnham

Bullying

Why do people bully?
Why do people tease?
Why do people kick and punch?
Why do people steal?
I feel sad and very lonely
Why do people laugh at my long hair?
I feel small and alone
it is so unfair
I am frightened and really hurt
I am bruised and very scared
I wish it would go away.

Sophie Croft (9)
Bentley Primary School, Farnham

The Animals' Life

There once was a cat called Gus
Who loved to ride in his bus,
The engine fell out
On a roundabout,
The poor little cat called Gus.

Gus' little friend called Dart
Loved to ride in his cart,
His pony tripped over
And ate a clover,
That dog who rode in a cart.

Dart's little friend called Stitch
Accidentally fell in a ditch,
He squirmed round and round
And found one pound,
That lucky guinea pig called Stitch.

Stitch's little friend called Hammy
Loved to wear his jammies,
He snuggled up tight
But woke with a fright,
That scared little hamster called Hammy.

Rachel England (11), Pamela Warne & Bethany Seymour (10)
Bridestowe Primary School, Okehampton

The Schoolhouse Rap

This is a rap about my school
The kids are fun but the teachers ain't cool
We went to the beach and rode a mule
This is a rap about my school!

This is a rap about my school
We're allowed to run but there's too many rules
We've got a pitch and a brand new pool
This is a rap about my school!

Theo Barwood (10) & Sam Heron (11)
Bridestowe Primary School, Okehampton

School

School is fun
School is great
Especially what the cook makes
Cod, that's what I like with pasta
After dinner I work faster
My best friend is Leon
We love to play football, but he always wins!

Nathan Tomkins (7)
Bridestowe Primary School, Okehampton

At Home With Amelia

I'm in the garden, in the sandpit
Mum is home and starting to knit
Theo is going to babysit
And Dad is off to his keep-fit.

Amelia Barwood (7)
Bridestowe Primary School, Okehampton

School's Out!

School's out
Scream and shout!
Time to have some fun
Jump high! Reach for the sky!
Now it's time to run!

Ellie Stoneman & Georgia Ley (8)
Bridestowe Primary School, Okehampton

Derek The Dartmoor Tractor

My favourite tractor went up onto Dartmoor
There he saw a see-saw
And little elves playing on the floor
They were singing, 'See-saw Marjory Dawe!'

Brandon Horn (9)
Bridestowe Primary School, Okehampton

Being Silly

As happy as a clown
As smelly as socks
As silly as a bully
As gooey as sludge.

Danny Bartlett (8)
Green Wrythe Primary School, Carshalton

Mean Tigers

As enormous as an elephant
As strict as my mum
As silly as clowns.

Adam Swan & Harry Cooper (8)
Green Wrythe Primary School, Carshalton

Cold And Smelly

As smelly as a skunk
As freezing as ice
As tired as an octopus.

Charly Everritt (8)
Green Wrythe Primary School, Carshalton

Word Poem

As smelly as a sock
As happy as a rabbit
As funny as clowns.

Tyla Smith (7)
Green Wrythe Primary School, Carshalton

Calligrams

As gooey as gum
As silly as a clown
As boiling as the sun.

Aaron Gardner (8)
Green Wrythe Primary School, Carshalton

The Amazing Words

As sweet as a fruit
As hard as a wall
As soft as a pillow
As bouncy as a ball
As short as an ant.

Mayowa Odimayo (7)
Green Wrythe Primary School, Carshalton

Colourful Words

As peaceful as a pond
As happy as a clown
As spooky as a ghost
As boiling as the sun
As giant as a castle.

Amy Dunnell (7)
Green Wrythe Primary School, Carshalton

My School Poem

As boiling as the sun
As silly as a clown
As brainy as Miss Ives
As brave as Miss Gauci.

Angel Rose (8)
Green Wrythe Primary School, Carshalton

Different Poems

As boiling as the sun
As silly as a clown
As brainy as Miss Ives
As brave as Miss Gauci.

Maisie Vidler (7)
Green Wrythe Primary School, Carshalton

Being Lazy

As lazy as a lion
As happy as a clown
As brave as a lion
As boiling as the sun.

Georgia Knott (8)
Green Wrythe Primary School, Carshalton

The Race

As happy as the class
As brainy as a fish
As huge as a giant
As peaceful as the music.

Robson Walker (7)
Green Wrythe Primary School, Carshalton

My Poem

As tall as a tree
As small as feet
As boiling as fire.

Bradley Prowse (8)
Green Wrythe Primary School, Carshalton

My Fantastic Poem

As peaceful as bedtime
As brainy as Jade
As boiling as the sun
As brave as a knight.

Jade Walker (8)
Green Wrythe Primary School, Carshalton

Sergeant Cobb

Sergeant Cobb is just so mean
He is thin and tall and lean
He has a horse so big
It is fatter than a pig
He shouts like a rattle
As he rides into battle
He reloads his gun
Bullets shiny as the sun
Behind enemy lines
How his sword shines
He has no beard, he thinks they're weird
He sniffs blood in the air
A smell he cannot bear
He retreats back to base
At a tremendous pace.

Ollie House (9)
Horris Hill Preparatory Boarding School, Newbury

A Poem For Grandpa

Grandpa, he is so kind
We have him always in our minds.

When times are bad, when times are mad
He is always there to lend a hand.

He is so smiley, he is so glad
He has a mind like an elastic band.

He is warm inside, he has such a heart
His ideas are like little paper darts.

He's as colourful as a parrot and roars like a lion
He is such fun, he burns the sun.

Forever we will love him so
Never will we let him go.

Ollie Spence (10)
Horris Hill Preparatory Boarding School, Newbury

Bully Ben

I was bullied in the playground
I was bullied again
And thrown in the bin.

At assembly I was nudged by a boy
Called Ben who was ten
He did it again.

I told my friends to fight big Ben
Who was ten
So they fought Ben
One called Glen
Who let Ben go and said,
'That's the end of bully Ben, who is ten.'

Angus Mayes (8)
Horris Hill Preparatory Boarding School, Newbury

Everything

Robots are tall and short
Gliders are twisting and turning
Clouds are floating and white
My teacher is dark and strong
My friends are good and bad
My brother is silly and annoying
My sister is the same.

Dogs are small and cheeky
Fish are colourful and cute
Kings are grand and as rich as chocolate
Books are large and boring
Bananas are yellow and green
Snakes are long and hissy.

Arthur O'Kelly (8)
Horris Hill Preparatory Boarding School, Newbury

A Golden Eagle

A golden eagle glides swiftly through the sky
A newborn lamb is feeding on the grass
The eagle's sharp eye spots it, he dives down
Lets his talons out and picks up the newborn lamb
Swiftly he glides back into the air
Goes back to his babies
And breaks up the meat
Into morsels fit for four.

Tom Carter (8)
Horris Hill Preparatory Boarding School, Newbury

Sport

Sport is a bag of energy
Sport is a talented game of pace and skill
Sport is the burn of oxygen in your lungs
Sport is sweat trickling down your back
Sport is the bitter taste of oranges at half-time.

Sport is the smile of success and loss
Sport is the high five of a teammate
Sport is the huddle of your team ready for action
Sport is the handshake of an opponent
Sport is the roar of the crowd at full-time.

Luke Fairbairn (9)
Horris Hill Preparatory Boarding School, Newbury

My First Day

I am a new boy
I am waiting in the playground
A big boy comes over and raises me off the ground
I feel so frightened, I want to go home
I am stuck in this playground all alone.

The teacher rings the bell
I think I'm in Hell
I don't know where the classroom is
I don't know what to do
I don't have a clue!

Archie Watt & Toby Sallitt (8)
Horris Hill Preparatory Boarding School, Newbury

A Scary Night Out

I thought one night I should go for a hike
Then I was lost and I came to an open door
I heard some chanting,
'A lizard's tail, a bloody face
A crocodile's tongue from a muddy place.'
I was scared to death and ran home
All alone, thinking of a bone.

Freddie Fagan (8), Charlie Thornton & Angus McGregor (9)
Horris Hill Preparatory Boarding School, Newbury

A Car Poem

It zooms down at 70mph
It's as red as the sun with four gleaming golden wheels
A giant roaring engine
The reason the engine can roar so load
Is because the engine is in the back
And the back is more powerful.

Callum Youngman (7)
Lapford CP School, Crediton

Christmas Decorations

A green hand very spiky
Its boxes are hidden in brown
Poison red-blood balls
Leaves shimmer like silk.

Tariq Moxham (9)
Lapford CP School, Crediton

The Sound Collector

(Based on 'The Sound Collector' by Roger McGough)

A stranger called this morning
Dressed all in black and grey
Put every sound into a bag
And carried it away.

The silence of the night
The crunching noise a fox makes when he hunts
The barking of the dog.

The silence of the night
The barking of the dog
The rustling of the leaves in winter
When the breeze blows with whistling in your ear.

The rustling of a bush when the wind blows
The splashing of a puddle when someone steps in
The shouting of the children
The squealing of people when they slam doors
The scrunching of paper
The slamming of hatches.

Jonathan Mort (7)
Milton Mount School, Crawley

The Sound Collector

(Based on 'The Sound Collector' by Roger McGough)

A stranger called this morning
Dressed all in black and grey
Put every sound into a bag
And carried it away.

The revving of a car
The whistling of a blackbird
The snapping of the branches
The crying of a baby.

The humming of a hummingbird
The stirring of the bats
The shouting of the teacher
The chattering of the children.

The blowing of the wind
The popping of the toaster
The shushing of the teacher
The spring of the springs.

Zak Way (6)
Milton Mount School, Crawley

The Sound Collector

(Based on 'The Sound Collector' by Roger McGough)

A stranger called this morning
Dressed all in black and grey
Put every sound into a bag
And carried it away.

The vroom of the car
The hum of the hummingbird
The shushing of the teacher
The creaking of the door.

The crackling of the branches
The smashing of glass
The screeching of the door
The screeching of the cupboard.

The whistling of the wind
The bang of the drums
The squelching of the mud
The crying of a baby.

Joshua Shadbolt (6)
Milton Mount School, Crawley

The Sound Collector

(Based on 'The Sound Collector' by Roger McGough)

A stranger called this morning
Dressed all in black and grey
Put every sound into a bag
And carried it away.

The chugging of a train
The chirping of the blackbird
The swishing of the trees
The vrooming of the cars.

The screaming of the children
The music of an MP3 player
The scraping of shoes
The pitter-patter of rain.

The scraping of the pencils
The slamming of the cupboards
The banging of the drum
The snapping of the branches.

Jade Taylor (7)
Milton Mount School, Crawley

The Sound Collector

(Based on 'The Sound Collector' by Roger McGough)

A stranger called this morning
Dressed all in black and grey
Put every sound into a bag
And carried it away.

The vrooming of a car
The vrooming of a motorbike
The scrunching of the leaves
The breeze in the trees.

The squelching of the mud
The shouting of a teacher
The shushing of the children
The gurgling of the washing.

The popping of the toaster
The music of the radio
The snipping of the scissors
The crying of the baby.

Josh Young (7)
Milton Mount School, Crawley

The Sound Collector

(Based on 'The Sound Collector' by Roger McGough)

A stranger called this morning
Dressed all in black and grey
Put every sound into a bag
And carried it away.

The dripping of a tap
The creaking of the branch
The stamping of shoes
The crying of a baby.

The snorting of a moose
The swishing of grass
The beeping of the horn
The dropping of books.

Charlie Hough (7)
Milton Mount School. Crawley

Upside-Down Food

In an upside-down world:
Is vanilla ice cream hot?
Will florets of broccoli grow in deciduous trees?
Would sugar-snap peas be the size of a Premiership football?
And chips be healthy for me?

Would beef stew be made in a freezer
And dark chocolate taste salty like kippers?
Would cold chicken be eaten for breakfast
And carrots be planted in slippers?

Would pure water kill people like poison?
Is orange juice chewy and lumpy?
Would pork sausages be delicious raw
And spicy chilli be triangular and bumpy?

Benjamin Harvey (8)
Newton Ferrers CE Primary School, Newton Ferrers

Animals I Like

'Mum, look what I've brought home today
I've brought a snake round to play.'
With a hiss and a slither
It makes my mum shiver,
'I'm so sorry, but it cannot stay!'

'Mum, look what I've brought home today
I've brought a kitten round to play.'
With a scratch at the mouse
And fleas in the house,
'I'm so sorry, but it cannot stay!'

'Mum, look what I've brought home today
I've brought a guinea pig round to play.'
With a squeak and a crash
The vase goes smash,
'I'm so sorry, but it cannot stay!'

'Mum, look what I've brought home today
I've brought a lizard round to play.'
With a croak and a sprint
It really starts to stink,
'I'm so sorry, but it cannot stay!'

Erik Wilson (10)
Newton Ferrers CE Primary School, Newton Ferrers

Light

Light is the colour of the sun and the sea
Light is the symbol of God
Light tastes like vanilla ice cream
Light smells like dandelions and roses and wax burning
Light sounds like birds tweeting and girls playing
Light feels very sleepy because it's very soothing
Light looks like the wind blowing and swinging in the air
And the sun dazzling people's eyes
Light makes me feel like dancing.

Jack Rhead & Ruben Da Rocha (6)
Newton Ferrers CE Primary School, Newton Ferrers

Light

Light is the colour of a rainbow
Light is the symbol of God
Light tastes like white ice cream
Light smells like a smoky fire
Light sounds like crunchy chips
Light feels like happiness
Light looks like the white sky
Light makes me feel good.

Jack Lane (9) & Robert Stockdale (6)
Newton Ferrers CE Primary School, Newton Ferrers

Light

Light is the colour of the brilliant blazing sun
Light is a sign for joyful happiness
Light tastes like sweet strawberries tingling my taste buds
Light smells like appetising vanilla ice cream
Light sounds like twittering birds in the dazzling sun
Light makes me blazing hot.

Kiera Burrows & Alex Hepburn (7)
Newton Ferrers CE Primary School, Newton Ferrers

Light

Light is a graceful sunset fading behind the clouds
A glittering, glimmering Catherine wheel twirling in the pitch-black sky
The smell of fiery crimson embers soaring up above the houses
Joyful music dancing around the valley
Sizzling sausages and smoky kebabs tingling on my taste buds
All is perfect in this world!

Bella Fellows (8) & Katie Mabberley (7)
Newton Ferrers CE Primary School, Newton Ferrers

Light

Light is a happy memory dancing around our heads
Lit-up Christmas trees dazzling on the dark nights
The scent of fresh strawberries in the bright summer sun
Birds chirping merrily in the bitter morning breeze
Tasty chocolate ice cream with a chocolate flake on top
All is light and cosy in the world.

Alice Epps (7) & Emma Phillips (8)
Newton Ferrers CE Primary School, Newton Ferrers

Light

Light is the colour of the sun glistening on the water
Light is a sparking shining star above us
Light tastes like smooth melting chocolate and ice cream
Light smells like sweet strawberries and new beginnings
Light sounds like birds singing in the hot, bright summer sun
Light feels like an old cuddly teddy in my bed
Light looks like humungous green leaves growing on the trees
Light makes me feel joyful.

Jessie Hill (7) & Rachel Bradley (8)
Newton Ferrers CE Primary School, Newton Ferrers

Light

Light is the colour of a rainbow
Light is juicy tasty strawberries
Light smells like a fresh breeze
Light sounds like birds tweeting merrily in the rustling trees
Light looks like a powerful Earth
Light makes me feel fresh and playful.

Tali Rodgers & Freya Butler (6)
Newton Ferrers CE Primary School, Newton Ferrers

Light

Light is the colour of large, juicy red strawberries growing on the trees
Light tastes like a huge, tasty yellow banana
Light is a massive ball of gas in the sky
Light smells like huge smoky barbecues
Light sounds like tiny birds tweeting happily in the huge green trees
Light looks like children splashing in the big blue sea
Light makes me feel happy.

Sam Bradley & Henry Christell (6)
Newton Ferrers CE Primary School, Newton Ferrers

Light

Light is the colour of delicious ice cream
Light is delightful joyful people
Light tastes like a huge, trickling, chocolate chip ice cream
Light smells like the fresh air outside
Light sounds like birds chirping happily in the morning
Light makes me feel ecstatic, joyful and playful
Light looks like golden leaves on the branches of trees
Light makes me move!

Matthew Gilbury & Jenny Guy (7)
Newton Ferrers CE Primary School, Newton Ferrers

Light

Light is the colour of dazzling flowers in the springtime
Light is glossy and charming
Light tastes like chilly ice cream
Light smells like roses in the shining sun
Light sounds like birds squawking
Light makes me feel relaxed on the seashore
Light looks like a steaming yellow ball
Light makes me wake up early on a sunny morning.

Joanne Woodlock & Bethany Coles (7)
Newton Ferrers CE Primary School, Newton Ferrers

Light

Light is the colour of juicy lemons
Light is yellow and shiny like the bright sun
Light tastes like sweet juicy lollipops and ice cream
Light sounds like peaceful sleeping in the garden
Light feels like sunbathing on the beach
Light looks like the beautiful blue sky and shiny blue sea
Light makes me feel joyful and relaxed.

India Da Rocha (7) & Harry Smith (8)
Newton Ferrers CE Primary School, Newton Ferrers

Light

Light is the colour of dolphins' skin as they leap joyfully through
the slippery waves
Light is the warm and cosy sun
Light tastes like sweet juicy lemons
Light smells like fresh minty grass swaying in the breeze
Light sounds like zebras running freely in the wild
Light feels like surfboarding on the shiny sea
Light looks like goodness
Light makes me happy!

Tom Wooderson & Ollie White (7)
Newton Ferrers CE Primary School, Newton Ferrers

Light

Light is the colour of a burning ball of fire
Light tastes like hot, steamy, frothy milk
Light sounds like the sun dancing in the daytime sky
Light feels like a new beginning
Light makes me feel cosy inside
Light makes me feel magnificent.

Romilly Carrick (6) & Bill Hussell (8)
Newton Ferrers CE Primary School, Newton Ferrers

The Life Of A Clam

I started off life the size of a grain of sand
And grew till I was as large as a man's hand.

I travelled all the world's seas
But the land has still evaded me.

I remember once I was washed ashore
On a tropical beach and there I saw

Two children digging a hole with some spades
And the remains of a razor shell's blades.

I am as old as the ocean and land put together
And have survived the harshest weather.

Now I have seen all the seas, all seven
I think I'll go to rest in seashell heaven.

Alice Donnellan (10)
Our Lady & St Patrick's RC Primary School, Teignmouth

King Shell

I am the emperor of the ocean
King of the deep blue sea
I have piercing sharp edges
For a shark launched its teeth into me
My life has been long, 60 million years at least
Although I'm still quite handsome
My face is beginning to crease
I'm starting to get old
So I'll make my way to shore
For I've lived a long and happy life
Deep down on the ocean floor.

Ellena Lumb (10)
Our Lady & St Patrick's RC Primary School, Teignmouth

The Shell Necklace

Once many years ago a sailor sailed off to sea
He took with him his jolly crew and his love maiden, Marie.

He gave to her a beautiful gift, a necklace of pearly colours
A shell on a smooth tight string, this necklace was truly spectacular!

Then one night a storm crept up on the ship and the wind
began to howl
And the waves started to swallow the ship like a lion on the prowl.

The crew tried all they could to battle the treacherous sea
But nothing could fight this monster, this ship was not meant to be.

All of a sudden, the monster took its last strike and knocked
the sailor's love down
Down, down, down, into the deep, dark sea.

The sailor shrieked a curse to the sky as he dived to the depths below
But Marie was stuck, her foot was caught, her life was about to go.

Time was running out, the sailor could not hold his breath
So he kissed his love one last time before she fell to her death.

Now I lie here locked in a glass cabinet on display for all to see
And next to me is the story of that stormy night and the loss
of maiden Marie.

Emily White (11)
Our Lady & St Patrick's RC Primary School, Teignmouth

Inside A Coffin

C offins are darker than tombs underground
O ver the hills, deep under, you will find one near
E nlightening things have happened
F ilthy clothes now rotting
I n a coffin
N ot open again
S eeing them never again.

Callum Pollock (9)
Pangbourne Primary School, Reading

Cat In The Window

'Cat in the window what do you hear?'
'George on the phone somewhere near
Jamie playing with his cars
Millie on her electric guitar
Nanny sleeping in her chair.'

'Cat in the window what do you hear?'
'Jamie singing nursery rhymes
Church bells ringing, sound like chimes
Mummy ironing all the clothes
Daddy doing what no one knows.'

Cat in the window what do you hear?'
'Everyone going to bed
So now lay down your weary head
Goodnight!'

Georgia Scott (10)
Pangbourne Primary School, Reading

The Pumpkin

The orange on the pumpkin
Is as bright as the fiery sun
The teeth on the pumpkin
Are as sharp as a machete blade
The nose of the juicy pumpkin
Is as big as a staircase
The juicy pumpkin itself
Is as menacing as a piranha
The candle of the pumpkin
Is as furious
As a hot fire.

George Needham (10)
Pangbourne Primary School, Reading

The Rusty Battered Door
(Based on 'The Door' by Miroslav Holub)

Go and open the door
Maybe there's a war
it might be as loud as your TV on full blast . . .
But go and open the door.

Go and open the door
Maybe there's a bomb about to land on you
A really big one with lots of explosives . . .
But go and open the door.

Go and open the door
Maybe there's a tank coming to flatten you
A big green tank with a gun pointing at you . . .
But go and open the door.

Go and open the door
England might be winning the war
They could be winning by miles or they could be losing . . .
But go and open the door.

George Rimmer (9)
Pangbourne Primary School, Reading

The Cauldron

The cauldron is as black as the night
And the size of a volcano
But stinks like rotten eggs
For incantations, potions or even cooking
Frogs' legs, monkey tail or lizard tongue
Not a wonder to the untrained eye
But, it's a cauldron full of *spells and surprises!*

Bryn Fray (9)
Pangbourne Primary School, Reading

My Magic Box

(Inspired by 'Magic Box' by Kit Wright)

In my magic box . . .
There is a white horse which I ride.

In my magic box . . .
There is a flying carpet that takes me on all sorts of adventures.

In my magic box . . .
There is a beautiful sunset over the sea.

In my magic box . . .
There is a wonderful garden filled with all my favourite flowers.

In my magic box . . .
There is a fabulous red velvet dress.

In my magic box . . .
There are all my friends.

In my magic box . . .
There is a chocolate fountain.

In my magic box . . .
There is a house filed with balloons.

Chloe Drewitt (10)
Pangbourne Primary School, Reading

Sent To Bed

My parents were very cross with me and sent me to bed
I'm very glad I didn't break anything, I only bumped my head.

But my brother broke his arm they put it in a sling
We went to the hospital, it was a silly thing.

Then we called the doctor and asked if he was OK
The doctor shouted, 'Oh no he's not, he doesn't want to play!'

At last we got out of the house and all piled in the car to visit
my annoying brother,
'What a horrible day we've had,' sighed our mother.

Loni Stephens (9)
Pangbourne Primary School, Reading

The Sports Door

(Inspired by 'The Door' by Miroslav Holub)

Go and open the astroturf door
Maybe there's a football stadium
A football stadium as big as the world
A million seats like a red sea.

Go and open the locker door
Maybe there's a rugby pitch
Players rummaging in the wet weather
Playing in the mud like a herd of cows.

Go and open the pool door
Maybe there's a swimming gala
Diving dolphins dancing delicately in the pool
Splashing water everywhere as they speed past!

Go and open the arena door
Maybe there's a cricket field
Children playing in the sun
The score is really very close.

Hopefully, I could do all of this
And maybe even more.

Reid Brown (10)
Pangbourne Primary School, Reading

Pollution

P eople are dumping rubbish
O n the riverside, it gets on my nerves
L akes are looking like rubbish tips
L ights are being left on wasting electricity
U nnoticing what you are doing
T he ice in the Arctic and Antarctica is melting
I n America jungles are disappearing
O dour is getting strong by the hour
N ow is the time to act, *today!*

Joshua Young (9)
Pangbourne Primary School, Reading

Bonfire Night

Whoosh went the firework
Crackle went a sparkler
Bonfire Night is the best!

Bang, the biggest firework ever
Sizzle went the sizzling sausages
Bonfire Night is the best!

Boom went the noisiest firework
Miaow went the frightened cats, how they hate fireworks
Bonfire Night is the best!

The fireworks are finished
People are going home
Everyone has enjoyed it!

Henry Penman (9)
Pangbourne Primary School, Reading

Easter

E aster is coming
A nimals are having babies
S ummer is near
T he hunt is on
E veryone is having fun
R abbits are hopping about

E ggs are being laid
G azing on the fields
G oodbye to the snow
S pring is here!

Katie Lewis (10)
Pangbourne Primary School, Reading

A Cosy Night In

As you snuggle up on the sofa, the fire flickers and rises
You enjoy a nice cup of steaming tea with crispy custard creams
Grab a duvet fresh from the tumble dryer
And sink your head into a cushion
Take spoonfuls of mouth-watering soup and crunch crusty bread
A warm cotton dressing gown with long violet ribbons
Two fluffy slippers in the shape of poodle dogs
As you snuggle up on the sofa, the fire flickers.

Nicole Carslake (9)
Pangbourne Primary School, Reading

The Crying Cat

Circles in and out of my legs
His tail tickles around my feet
His eyes gleam like stars in the sky
His favourite dinner
Scared away under the dark sky
The cat stares at me like it hasn't been fed for months
The cat hisses at me as loud as a rattlesnake
I turn and stare at the beautiful cat
I am petrified!

Callum Wilkins (9)
Pangbourne Primary School, Reading

Easter Bunny

E *aster is here!*
A nimals come out to play
S un shines brightly in the sky
T he children are getting excited
E aster eggs are hidden somewhere
R abbits running all around

B old and beautiful Easter eggs
U neaten eggs melting in the sun
N uts are being eaten by squirrels
N obody is sad at Easter time
Y oung and old gather together at Easter!

Sophie Guyon (10)
Pangbourne Primary School, Reading

Werewolf

The moon is full, the werewolf howls
The farmers are scared from the missing cows
Blink and blink again
What is missing?
What is wrong?
Wait a minute, the farmer's gone!
All that's left is bloodstained grass
And a shotgun made of brass
A crooked hand grabs the handle
It all goes dark like a blown-out candle
The deadliest creature with a shotgun
Killed as mach as a ton.

Solomon Davis (10)
Pensans Commuity Primary School, Penzance

Ten Billion Phones

There was a young girl called Morgan Jones
And she had ten billion phones
She gave one to Max, she gave one to Ben
But they gave her back a big fat hen.

She gave one to Mum and she gave one to Dad
But they said they were very, very bad
She tried her cousin and she tried her aunt
But they just said they really can't.

She gave one to her dog and she gave one to her fish
But they gave her a liquorice
She tried her friend Josh and she tried her friend Tamsin
But when she asked them for tea, they just walked straight in.

She was busy all day getting rid of those phones
And this is her name, Morgan Jones.

Morgan Jones (9)
Pensans Commuity Primary School, Penzance

Animals

Cats are cute and cuddly
I used to have one called Polly
Now I have a dog called Holly
She's very nosy and jolly.

I used to have two goldfish
They were called Sylvester and Tweety
They were two little sweeties.

Foxes have amber eyes that shine in the moonlight
But lemurs are my favourite animals by far
They are the cutest with two, huge brown eyes.

So these are my favourite animals and pets
And when I'm older I want to be a vet.

Madeleine Ead (10)
Pensans Commuity Primary School, Penzance

I Am Cloe Carter

I am Cloe Carter
I am Cloe, I am funny
I have a rumbling tummy
I am as sweet as honey
I am scary
I am friendly
I'm as cheery as a cherry
I am as noisy as a pencil case
I have a pretty face.

Cloe Carter (9)
Pensans Commuity Primary School, Penzance

Dragons

Fire comes out of a dragon's red mouth
Some dragons eat us, but they don't think about their health
Dragons live in some dusty caves with dirty elf slaves
The slaves used to live in the sea and there used to be rough waves
All day the slaves weep
All day the slaves sleep.

Tamsin Weeks (9)
Pensans Commuity Primary School, Penzance

Something

It's as cheesy as the cheese with holes in
It draws me in like a seagull to rubbish
It's as toxic as an American wasteland
The colours are as dull as Simon Cowell
It's as creased as my boxer shorts.

They are so horrible as wind
They smell as bad as a fish sprinkled with oil
What is it?

Jake Price (10)
Priory RC Primary School, Torquay

The Pencil

While the pencil jiggles about
It rolls left to right
And when it starts to write
It never wants to stop.

Its favourite thing it likes
Is to write poems every single night
And when I have homework
It helps without a sigh.

My pencil is the best pencil
Because it is not the same
Like any other pencil
That I have ever seen.

It's my pencil
But most of all
it's my best pencil.

Luchia Valenti   (10)
Priory RC Primary School, Torquay

Muscles

I keep on working
I never stop
Until you are as dead as a used mop
You should keep me healthy and give me my lunch
Because without me, you can't move much
So keep me well watered and keep me well fed
So late in the night you can snuggle your ted
And when you wake up the next morning to eat
Just remember what is propelling your feet
It's me, of course, wonderful I am
As awesome as an eagle landing on the sand.

Nicholas Stott   (10)
Priory RC Primary School, Torquay

The Puppy

She's as small as a toy car
And looks at me as if I'm her only friend
She's as bouncy as a ball
And as brown as chocolate.

She plays with me, night and day
And is as soft as a teddy bear
She's as light as a feather
And as cute as anything you've ever seen
She's as special as the world to me
And she is my best friend.

She runs as fast as lightning
And I love her so much
She is so playful
And she's the best puppy in the world.

Jade Harris (10)
Priory RC Primary School, Torquay

The Ocean

The ocean was as calm as the blue sky
And as glistening as a crystal
The waves were as strong as an ark
The sea colour was as blue as the shining night sky
And as sparkly as the stars
Even though the waves are still, gentle and calm
The ocean was as quiet as a pin drop
The boats moved side to side in the slight wind
The stars would reflect in the blue shining ocean.

Adelina Schiano (10)
Priory RC Primary School, Torquay

The London Eye

As I stretch my massive arms
The whistling winds through my grips
People come and go as I turn round
And round
Evening comes as I watch
The sun as it gently disappears
Behind Big Ben.

Morning comes once again
As children bounce around
I cry please stop or else
I'll break down
They come to see my
Good views
I love it when they're around.

Olivia Bickley (10)
Priory RC Primary School, Torquay

The Thing

It's as shiny as mildew on a blade of grass on an early winter's morning
It's as sharp as a blunt pencil
It's more deadly than a freshly sharpened dagger
It's faster than a Bugati Veyron
It steams like boiling water
And as hot as the molten core
You can easily bend it into shapes
But you can normally find it is quite hard
But no one knows what it is.

Jordan Leleivre (11)
Priory RC Primary School, Torquay

My Pencil

My pencil is like no other pencil
It wriggles and jiggles all day
I try to make it stop sometimes
But it just wants to play and play.

It skips and gallops all over the page
Like it's in a dance
I watch and stare, quite amazed
Just as if I'm in a trance.

It has got a mind of its own
If it's not writing, it's drawing
My eyes are on it all day
And if I am not staring, I'm gawping.

My pencil and I are now great friends
It's with me all day and night
Once, it drew a moustache on my face
In the morning I got quite a fright!

So that is the end of my pencil
We had a good time I must say
I got a new pen for Christmas
Now *that* just wants to play and play!

Lucy Jane Meacock (10)
Priory RC Primary School, Torquay

The Swan

As hungry as a monster
As white as snow
As I wiggle my tail everybody says, ahh
I've got wobbly legs like jelly
I see humans wearing wellies
I peck you for fun
I always eat buns
But most of all I look like you.

Danielle Lee (11)
Priory RC Primary School, Torquay

The Boulder

As heavy as an elephant
Stronger than a safe in a steel room
The size of a house
As rustic as a cliff edge from wave erosion
As rough as the skin under my heel
Quicker than lightning bolts
More deadly than a terrorist in action
Full of life.

William Nicolle (10)
Priory RC Primary School, Torquay

Emotions Poem

Happiness tastes as light as candyfloss, one of the pleasures of life
Sadness tastes like ash, a smouldering sensation in your mouth.

Love smells like strawberries, fresh and ripe
Hate smells like a roaring fire, the smoke choking your soul.

Trust feels like a glowing warmth, covering your body
Distrust feels like a sharp spear piercing your skin.

Courage is seen as impregnable armour protecting you from all
Fear is seen as humility preying on your brain.

Anger sounds like a thousand drums beating in your head
Joy sounds like the calm ocean and laughter all around.

James Nash (11)
St David's School, Purley

Feelings

Joy sounds like fireworks going off in front of you
Joy looks like a sunset in the summer
Joy smells like an egg and bacon breakfast
Joy tastes like a raspberry ripple ice cream
Joy feels like sliding down a water slide.

Courage sounds like someone gulping
Courage looks like eyes blinking in the dark
Courage smells like burnt toast
Courage tastes like garlic on my tongue
Courage feels like a bully's breath in my face.

Natasha Phillips (10)
St David's School, Purley

The Rainbow Of Feelings

Scarlet is anger like an exploding volcano
Yellow is happiness like the burning smile of the sun
Pale blue is freedom like a cloudless sky
Navy is sadness like dropping down into the depths of despair
Gold is courage like the person who stands out in the crowd
Black is fear like dropping down a never-ending black hole
White is love like a graceful dove
Your favourite colour is joy
Mine being pink, an enormous flock of flamingos.

Emily Jones (11)
St David's School, Purley

Anne's Poem

Anne was a happy, lively girl from the family of Frank.
But when Hitler came into power, Anne's heart sank.
They knew if they stayed in Germany they wouldn't last the day,
So they decided that, as quick as they could, they would run away.
In Amsterdam she had lots of fun and loved her new school,
But Anne knew she wasn't safe in Amsterdam, she was no fool.
Germany soon attacked and began to thrive
The Frank family went into hiding to save their lives.
The hideout was in Prisengracht behind a warehouse,
desks and chairs.
The family tried to take with them everything that was theirs.
Two years they spent inside the Annexe, all cold and musty
With the scraping sound of rats on the floorboards, all hard and dusty,
Inside their little hiding place they were safe from German reign.
But they were captured and taken away to German trucks and trains
They could have survived the war, but it was not to be,
After eighteen months of pain and suffering Anne died in captivity.
Anne dreamed of fame and fortune but died because she was sick.
Her diary was published, she got fame and fortune but was gone -
isn't that ironic?

Miles Edwards (11)
St John's Meads CE Primary School, Eastbourne

The Sun Gives You A Shadow

The sun gives you a shadow
The shadow follows you everywhere you go!

When you go to a friend's house, it goes with you
Your friend has a shadow too, when you play, it plays too.

When you cuddle your friend
Your friend's shadow cuddles too.

Tom Roberts (7)
St John's Meads CE Primary School, Eastbourne

The Circle Of Light

The light goes around the bulb
And soon it will run out
This room gets black and dark
it's spooky and hard to see!

You have to get a torch
And find another bulb
And soon that bulb will run out
The circle of light begins again!

Max Marshall (7)
St John's Meads CE Primary School, Eastbourne

Monday's Child

Monday's child is a funny bunny
Tuesday's child really likes the sunny
Wednesday's child has a spotty potty
Thursday's child has a horse called Lotty
Friday's child is very lazy
Saturday's child is very crazy
And the child that is born on the Sabbath day
Is lazy all day.

Sasha Vieira (7)
St John's Meads CE Primary School, Eastbourne

Monday's Child

Monday's child has a spotty potty
Tuesday's child is called Lottie
Wednesday's child is a funny bunny
Thursday's child is as good as gold
Friday's child is very mouldy
Saturday's child is like a botty
Sunday's child likes to make lots of noise.

Phoebe Hepburn (7)
St John's Meads CE Primary School, Eastbourne

Monday's Child

Monday's child is fat and lazy
Tuesday's child finds a daisy
Wednesday's child plays with Maisie
Thursday's child is twice the size
Friday's child is very wise
Saturday's child is full of lies
And the child that's born on the seventh day
Is like a big fat piece of *hay!*

Louis Wilson (7)
St John's Meads CE Primary School, Eastbourne

Monday's Child

Monday's child cries all day
Tuesday's child's birthday's in May
Wednesday's child runs through the house
Thursday's child caught a mouse
Friday's child has been sick
Saturday's child plays with a stick
And the seventh child has a fit!

Maddy Smith (7)
St John's Meads CE Primary School, Eastbourne

Monday's Child

Monday's child is kind and loving
Tuesday's child is quite stunning
Wednesday's child is learning fast
Thursday's child is coming last
Friday's child is reading books
Saturday's child always has looks
But the child that is born on the Sabbath day
Is loving, stunning . . . and a pain in the neck!

Sophie Lucas (8)
St John's Meads CE Primary School, Eastbourne

Monday's Child - Don't Be Bad

Monday's child is big and bad
While Tuesday's child smells like Dad
Wednesday's child just goes mad
Thursday's child wears a wig
Friday's child looks like a pig
Saturday's child, *'Oh no, don't open that lid.'*
Sunday's child, a guest is he, but he does not take interest in me.

Stan Garbett (8)
St John's Meads CE Primary School, Eastbourne

Monday's Child . . .

Monday's child is a spotty potty
Tuesday's child is called Lotty
Wednesday's child is a funny bunny
Thursday's child is as good as gold
Friday's child is very good
Saturday's child is having a birthday
And the child that is born on the seventh day
Is the noisy one, OK?

Mary Oakenfold (8)
St John's Meads CE Primary School, Eastbourne

The Penniless Orphans

The poor children think they are worthless
They eat food that makes them skinny
The uneducated children want to go to school, but can't
The boys sit in the dirty ground, hot and tired.

They sit miserable and angry
They stink as they don't wash
The penniless orphans are exhausted
After a long day at work; but don't get anything
They are feeling broken-hearted.

They're treated like dirt under the hot sun
They work all day and get nothing
Which they find unfair.

Jordan Appleyard (11)
St John's Primary School, Woking

The Poor Children!

The children suffer in the hot steamy weather
They have *no* food
Penniless
The kids are very tired because they have been working all day long
But only work for a tiny bit of money
Unfair
They are very hungry and worn out
Picking food for other people, but not themselves
Starved
They have to go barefoot also
They could really hurt their feet very badly
They're unhealthy
Devastating.

Abbey Palmer (11)
St John's Primary School, Woking

Child Labour

All tired and weary
Sad and upset
Hungry for food, that's what they said.

Hard work is labour
Do it now or face the consequences
Thirsty and downhearted for the rest of their life.

All pain, no sleep
And no joy for them
Their lives are being destroyed.

Someone can help them
But who could it be?
Could it be me or is it you who can help them?

A little house
A little bed
And so little time to go inside with family.

Heavy baskets to carry
To get home in time
You need to rush and hopefully make it.

Ryan Cree (11)
St John's Primary School, Woking

Child Labour

Untreated, tired and cold, they don't know what to do to please people
Despite being hurt and hungry, they still work for their families
It's disgraceful.

The hungry unloved children work all day
Scared that they haven't done enough work
It's upsetting.

Just like them, most children don't have an education
Their future is peeling food and collecting water
Who can help them?

Bethany Westwood (10)
St John's Primary School, Woking

Poor Children

The children look sad
They feel hungry
They are miserable, wistful and tired
They can't take another day.

They need to be loved because they are unloved
They need to have water because they are parched
They need shelter because they are roasting in the scorching heat

They have no money to live
They are so unlucky
I wish I could help.

Lacey Meredith (10)
St John's Primary School, Woking

My Father

I am a young girl, my name is Hannah
I live with my mother and of course my nana
I also have a father
He is rather weird in ways
But he did do something that caught my eye
A silly dance that he called 'Hello and Goodbye'.

He tries to make me laugh but it doesn't work at all
He has been telling me the same jokes
Since I was very small
He doesn't realise I now know every one.

I wish he would come back home to live with us like before
Then Nana could go back to Scotland and I wouldn't hear her moan,
'Clean your room Hannah,'
'Wash the dishes Hannah,'
'Be kind to your mother Hannah'
'It will all get easier soon Hannah.'

Claire Martin (9)
St Thomas Garnet's School, Bournemouth

The Beach

I like going to the beach
Partly because it's easy to reach
Because we live right next to it
To lie down on it
To play on it
There's plenty of room to sit.

I like paddling in the sea
And on the promenade there's a quay
In both of them there's plenty to see
For shells to see
For shops to see
It all seems very much to me.

I like looking in rock pools
I like playing with beach balls
Usually the water's cool
The ice cream's cool
The wet sand's cool
What a nice change from school!

Nicholas Beaumont (10)
St Thomas Garnet's School, Bournemouth

An Ode To Harry Potter

Harry is smart and wise,
A cut above the other guys.
Ron is his best mate;
Together they meet their fate.
Their other friend is Hermione Granger;
The three of them face every danger.
For one enemy they all do share,
Voldemort who has no hair!
The final book I have not yet read,
I wonder who will end up dead?

Jeremy Sobisch (9)
St Thomas Garnet's School, Bournemouth

Calamity On The Farm

Calamity, calamity
The hens escaped from their cage
The cows are in the kitchen
The farmer's in a rage.

Calamity, calamity
Everything's gone wrong
The cockerel's in the dustbin
Singing his morning song.

Calamity, calamity
The pigs aren't in their sty
The sheep are running wild
I really don't know why.

Calamity, calamity
The baby's stuck in wire
The duck is being eaten
And the farmhouse is on fire!

Matthew Giddens (10)
St Thomas Garnet's School, Bournemouth

Where Am I From?

Excuse me, but where am I from?
I've been trying to find out for days
And even family won't tell me like my mum.

Am I from space
Or is it just because I have an alien's face?

Am I from Jupiter
Or is it just me getting stupider?

I've found out where I've come from now
I come from the heavenly angels
Oh look down there
I see some lovely heavenly bagels.

Gabriella St Clair-Hefler (9)
St Thomas Garnet's School, Bournemouth

My New Dog

I have a new puppy called Poppy.
She has ears that are all floppy.
Today she chewed up the toothpaste,
And that was such a waste.

Her fur was very silky and soft
Until she went up into the loft.
She came back down all covered in dust
And couldn't understand what was all the fuss!

I'm training her to sit and beg,
But instead she prefers to bite my leg.
I love her very much,
But she is driving me totally nuts!

Piers Verstage (9)
St Thomas Garnet's School, Bournemouth

My Family

There's seven in our family
My family's rather large
We have two playful puppies
And my mum *thinks* she's in charge.

Three children live in our house
I'm the eldest child
My little brother is only one
And my sister's rather wild!

Frankie Skinner (11)
St Thomas Garnet's School, Bournemouth

In The Days Of Winter

In the days of winter
Cold and frosty
Water becomes ice
And the trees are bare.

The spring sun is rising
And the snow melts from the ground
Many crops start to grow
With brightness all around.

The beach is a holiday
Eating ice cream in summer
Football at the park
And heat forever.

Dominic Hughes (10)
St Thomas Garnet's School, Bournemouth

Jed

I have a Scottie dog
And his name is Jed
Every single morning
He gets me out of bed.

This is very annoying
He does this to be fed
The best dog in the world
Is my dog Jed.

Matthew Thomson (11)
St Thomas Garnet's School, Bournemouth

One Moment In Spring

I stand outside in the blazing sun
And smell the fresh tender grass.

Beautiful flowers blossom out
Whilst bees suck the nectar out
In my back garden.

The sun beats down on my sweaty face
As ducks swim gracefully alongside the pond
Against the shining yellow daffodils.

Spring gives you a warm sensational feeling
I adore springtime.

Jean-Jacques Coppini (11)
St Thomas Garnet's School, Bournemouth

The Seaside

Of all the places that I like to be
My favourite is beside the sea.

I have to watch the waves that crash
They tumble down to make a splash.

I search for glistening scaly fish
To catch an eel is my greatest wish.

I dig and build on the soft yellow sand
A spade and bucket in my hand.

With a net clutched tight I search rock pools
It's time to go home when my mother calls.

Rebecca Giddens (10)
St Thomas Garnet's School, Bournemouth

Football

Shooting, saving, scoring
Winning, cheering, chanting
Nutmegs, goals, lobs
Chips, free kicks, penalties
Defending, striking, passing
Streakers, fans, mascots
Referees, managers, coaches
Happy, sad, exciting
Thrilling, boring, amazing
Throwing, corners, goal kicks
Fouling, tackling, arguing
Swearing, shouting, diving.

Diarmid Becker (11)
St Thomas Garnet's School, Bournemouth

My Dad's Great!

He does my work when I am late
And all the cooking too
He's grumpy in the morning
And plays his guitar on the loo
He reads to me, sings silly songs
They don't ever rhyme
He makes me do my homework
And go to bed on time
When my dad is off to work
He comes home very late
It's when he's not at home
I think my dad's great!

Georgia MacDonald-Taylor (9)
St Thomas Garnet's School, Bournemouth

Yuck, Yuck, Yuck

Whenever my mum gives me a kiss on the cheek
I say, 'Yuck, yuck, yuck.'
Whenever I have mouldy cheese sandwiches
I say, Yuck, yuck, yuck.'
It's always yuck, yuck, yuck.
Whenever I walk down the road and I see cat poo
I say, 'Yuck, yuck, yuck.'
Whenever I see my sister kiss her boyfriend
I say, 'Yuck, yuck, yuck.'
But whenever I see her kiss her lovely cake
I want to join in.

Kira Allum (8)
St Thomas Garnet's School, Bournemouth

Rushing Through The Trees

Over the hills I go
With a pair of broken skis
Rushing through the trees
The snow is turning red
I think I'm almost dead
Next thing I know
I'm in hospital with stitches in my head.

Joshua Allum (10)
St Thomas Garnet's School, Bournemouth

Best

Don't mess with the best
Because the best don't mess
So always try your best with the rest
And always clean your mess
But don't be bossy with the best
And be always the same as the rest.

Rosheen Daly (8)
St Thomas Garnet's School, Bournemouth

Jasmine

Jasmine is in my room
And outside of my window
Every day she opens out
All the time she smells as good as blossom

She needs a drink of water once a day
If you don't, she may die
I must ask her if she can see you
It's Grandma's favourite and mine
It's the sweet-smelling flower, jasmine.

Katherine Brereton (11)
St Thomas Garnet's School, Bournemouth

Little Hamster

Some hamsters run away but my one doesn't
My hamster likes playing hide-and-seek with me
My hamster likes sleeping
When he wakes up, he explores his breakfast
My hamster loves spinning on his wheel
I really like my hamster.

Nikan Houshmand-Motlagh (7)
St Thomas Garnet's School, Bournemouth

Splashing

Me and my mummy
Playing in the back garden
Having so much fun.

Splashing in the swimming pool
Getting nice and wet
Diving under the water
Jumping up and down
Shooting hoops into the net.

Scott Austin (8)
St Thomas Garnet's School, Bournemouth

Left, Right

Left, right
Left, right
That's what the band sings out
At night.

Left, right
Left, right
The band's clothes
Are very bright.

Left, right
Left, right
The band say they have
Lots of might.

Left, right
Left, right
Why can't they
Go to sleep at night?

Joseph Yeadon (9)
St Thomas Garnet's School, Bournemouth

Anger

Anger is homework
Anger is school
Anger is football
Anger is reading
Anger is maths
Anger is spelling
Anger is brothers
Anger is Barbies
Anger is *annoying mums*
Anger is *this!*

Eva Becker (8)
St Thomas Garnet's School, Bournemouth

On The Seabed

On the seabed there are many things
Rocks, coral and crabs
The fish that swish by
Are colours of pink or blue
Green or red
But don't forget above the seabed
There are many dangers that lurk
But on the sand you're safe and sound
With the cold wisp of wind.

Eleanor Austin (11)
St Thomas Garnet's School, Bournemouth

The Christmas Lunch

When Mum makes the most delicious turkey
There's always something wrong with it
And when my sister opens the biggest present
She's so carried away that she forgets to eat her lunch
But when my cousin comes round, she says, 'Ugh!'
Mum marches off into the smelly kitchen
But I think Mum tries really hard.

Lucy Taylor (7)
St Thomas Garnet's School, Bournemouth

The Sleepover

A sleepover makes me happy
My friends and I play games
I love it when we whisper secrets
Under the covers
We share our midnight feast
In the morning Mum comes to wake us up
But we go straight under the covers.

Gina Davis (7)
St Thomas Garnet's School, Bournemouth

My Brother

My brother is funny
He bounces like a bunny.

When he flies a kite
He says, 'I'm so high I swear I could fly.'

He is kind and gentle
When I hear him read.

He plays in his room very calmly
But his room is very balmy.

He is as funny as can be
When I say, 'Hi everyone, I'm a bumblebee!'

Lily Newton (8)
St Thomas Garnet's School, Bournemouth

Animal Types

A n animal such as a cat makes me happy
N ice animals are the ones I would like to stroke
I ce animals are the ones that live in the Arctic
M ammals feed their babies by themselves
A nimals are sometimes soft
L and is home to quite a lot of animals

T igers are meant to be mean and horrible
Y our pet could be soft and cuddly
P ets are mostly soft, not all pets are soft
E lephants live in Africa and India
S nakes are sometimes poisonous.

Sophie Sawyer (8)
St Thomas Garnet's School, Bournemouth

My Sister And Me In Italy

Up a mountain in a cable car
Up a volcano to see so far
Around Pompeii we walked
At lunch we listened as the waiters talked.

Down to Amalfi
On a bus we chugged
Fruit and cheese
From the market we lugged.

Pizza and pasta
We gobbled with glee
When the sun shone
We swam in the sea
My sister and me.

Eleanor Riches (9)
Sandcross School, Reigate

Snow

I stared at it
I just couldn't resist it
I dived . . .
Soft and fluffy
Cold and cuddly
Every different emotion
I was sinking
Deeper and deeper
It surrounded me
I stretched out
My arms as angel wings
It embraced me.

Harriet Wood (9)
Sandcross School, Reigate

Before Creation

Before creation when the sky was red and the stars twinkled like jewels
The sun was snow-white and the planets were round, round
                                                          like precious pearls.

The sun aged and found its time was almost nigh
After years of light it finally gave way to the vortex of the sky
In a flash of light the black hole was born and the planets entered
                                                          the void.

The future of the universe, the future of years to come
Was held by a tiny black speck.

For this black speck was all that was left
Born from a shining white sun
Resting in a blood-red sky
Millions of tiny particles littered the sky with unearthly beauty.

And so the universe was created and here we are
We have come so far
What will happen in the next billion years?

Daisy Moon (10)
Sandcross School, Reigate

The Eel

This way, that way
Up and down
Round and round
He's not from town.

A murderous creature
From the deep
If you're brave enough
Have a peep.

Sharp and sly
Never frail
Then, he's out of here
With a flick of his tail.

Georgie Coram (10)
Sandcross School, Reigate

Friendship

Friendship appears big and strong, then disappears in tears.
They appear here and disappear there,
Like day and night,
Like birds in flight,
Like snowflakes on the ground,
But you and I are something different,
Our friendship's never-ending,
Like blue sky and mountains high,
It will never go away.

Eleanor Burford (9)
Sheet Primary School, Petersfield

Wouldn't It Be Strange

Wouldn't it be strange,
If the house were made of plastic?
Wouldn't it be strange,
If the trees were made of rubber?
Wouldn't it be strange,
If the boys were made of skulls?
Wouldn't it be strange,
If the girls were made of flowers?
Wouldn't it be strange,
If our head was blue?
Wouldn't it be strange,
If our hand was pink
And it flushed down the loo?
Wouldn't it be strange,
If we had no eyes?
Wouldn't it be strange,
If humans lived under water
And sea creatures lived on land?

William Price (7)
Sherwell Valley Primary School, Torquay

A Bowling Alley In Space

Have you ever heard of a bowling alley in space,
Where aliens come to play?
They love and they laugh,
Whilst sitting at the bar,
Which is wrapped right around Mars.

While they play they drink green, fizzy pop,
Which bubbles in their mouths.
They say *yum* when they drink it,
They say it's healthy for their gums.

I'd like to live in space and go bowling every day,
But I don't wish to be an alien,
I think I will be an astronaut!

Martha Downs (8)
Sherwell Valley Primary School, Torquay

The Upside-Down Poem

I eat a chocolate bar upside-down
My brother plays football on his hands
My teacher teaches me when it's dark
And I go to sleep in the day

The sky is made of water
The sea is made of air

I learn about everything
But everything is nonsense
Plants that grow downwards
And teeth that go ting

The children teach the teachers
Will the teachers listen or chat?
Will the children teach about nothing?

Amy Potter (7)
Sherwell Valley Primary School, Torquay

The Funny Things In Space

Whoosh, whoosh, go Saturn's spinning rocks,
Whizz, bang, the rocket is landing,
Spinning Earth going around
Is the sun going *boom?*

I see a moon alien,
Whizz, boom, sizzle,
I see fireworks.
Ting, ping, go the stars,
It is just like a show!

Crackle, snap, wow, a big meteor,
Tick, tick, the time goes,
Whoosh, go dazzling shooting stars.
Bing, bong, I see a fluffy white planet,
Let's go!

Angel Harper (7)
Sherwell Valley Primary School, Torquay

How Strange

I was walking up the street,
When I saw a flower eating a sweet!
'How peculiar,' I said that day.
But then I heard a horse go *neigh!*
The next day I walked up a lane,
Now here comes an animal without a name.

Everyday I see a different animal,
But I don't know why.
I want to ask them, but I don't know how.
Maybe is should ask the weird looking cow!

Izzy Huddart (8)
Sherwell Valley Primary School, Torquay

Isn't It Weird

One night, when I didn't hear chatting,
I didn't walk up the stairs to not listen,
I didn't see a man wearing a lady's dress
And I didn't see a lady wearing a man's suit!

No, no, no! this can't be right,
Things have got ever so weird.
Why can't life be just normal?
Why is everything weird?

Amelia Simpson (7)
Sherwell Valley Primary School, Torquay

Giraffe

The grass was very green,
The very, very luscious grass was swaying in the breeze.
The trees were enormous,
The yellow flowers were very colourful.
The elegant giraffe was huge, enormous!

Tierney Leaver (7)
Sherwell Valley Primary School, Torquay

Very Funny Indeed

Wouldn't it be funny if the sky was green
And the animals spotty and yellow?
Wouldn't it be?

Wouldn't it be funny if the homes were small
And you couldn't get through the window?
Wouldn't it be?

Would it be funny if the clouds were pink?
Wouldn't it be hilarious if rhymes were ended with ink?

Laurie Ahearne (7)
Sherwell Valley Primary School, Torquay

Colourful Leaves

The hot summer's tree, still in its same place,
Orange leaves falling from the trunk.
Branches swaying from side to side,
Pigeons singing, blue tits screaming
Because the sky is huge.

Children shouting around the tree,
Grass growing under the big tree,
Leaves start to grow,
As orange leaves fall off.

James Campbell (8)
Sherwell Valley Primary School, Torquay

The Rain Goes Down The Drain

The rain goes down the drain
In a gushing type of way
And goes gurgle, rushing down fast.

The rain is misery,
Making splashing puddles,
Rain puddles are fun!

Louis Egan (8)
Sherwell Valley Primary School, Torquay

What It Is Like At School

I'm always getting into things,
And instruments always go ting,
But here comes the great big bully,
He always active and fully,
Here comes the teacher,
As bossy as can be,
Next up we're having tea, with a bumblebee!

Adam Smith (8)
Sherwell Valley Primary School, Torquay

Animal Move

Here we are in Slug Street
There's slugs everywhere, with no feet!

Next we're in Cheetah Land
But for some reason there's loads of sand!

Then we see a crocodile,
It's swimming down the River Nile!

Every animal makes a move
And where there's music they do a groove!

Lloyd Higgins (7)
Sherwell Valley Primary School, Torquay

Football Poem

Steven Gerrard was running down the pitch,
Fell into a big, black ditch,
Steven Gerrard passed it to Ashley Cole,
Who scored a great goal!
Rooney passed it to Owen,
The crowd's response was really glowing!

Kieran Moore (7)
Sherwell Valley Primary School, Torquay

Autumn Tree

Red leaves sitting on the ground
Brown sticks lying around.
Black background looking
At the colourful tree standing.

Dark trunk standing
On the green leaf pile blowing.

Dark log balancing
Right next to the dark tree, standing.

Sam Davies (8)
Sherwell Valley Primary School, Torquay

Season's Ending

Watery snow standing
Icy houses clattering
Glowing lights flickering
Cold people playing
Blooming flowers spreading
Emerald grass growing
Scuttling bugs running
Bouncing bunnies hopping
Hot sun shining
Glowing fireflies flying
Glistening leaves swirling
Crinkly leaves falling
Little people playing
Still trees standing
Tall branches snapping.

Lizzie Rodda (7)
Sherwell Valley Primary School, Torquay

The Grumpy Teacher

There was once a grumpy teacher,
Who was a bit of a preacher,
Who lived in a house,
With a tiny, old mouse,
who turned into a big creature.

Max Robinson (8)
Sherwell Valley Primary School, Torquay

Wouldn't It Be Funny

Wouldn't it be funny if a plant could shut the door?
And the door could sing?
And the sky was pink and the clouds could snap at you?
Wouldn't it be funny if a tree could walk?
And a curtain said whoosh?

Naomi Wilson (8)
Sherwell Valley Primary School, Torquay

Frozen Ice

Sugary snow asleep
emerald trees spiking
chestnut twigs freezing
icy ponds glittering
frozen children playing
galloping deer running
bouncing rabbits hopping
bronze log cabin frozen
flying birds whirling
red fire burning.

Freya Woods (7)
Sherwell Valley Primary School, Torquay

The Snowy Lodge

Snowy lodge standing
tall trees shivering
white snow falling
deep snow growing
green plants dying
grey clouds moving
misty windows freezing
bright lights shining
plain roof lazing
patterned tracks fading.

Felix Nicholls (8)
Sherwell Valley Primary School, Torquay

Jake The Baker

There was an old man called Jake
Who really liked to bake
So he bought an egg
From his friend Meg
And went to make his cake.

Bethany England (7)
Sherwell Valley Primary School, Torquay

Snow Time

Sugary snow falling
Icy treetops blowing
White rooftops frozen
Big white cottage
Tall trees swaying
Frozen, slippery stairs
Bright lights flashing
Little icy bits
Cold people ice skating
Old white window sills freezing
Hot flames burning.

Ame Toms
Sherwell Valley Primary School, Torquay

The Snowy Winter

Fluffy white snow
Green trees swaying
Hot chocolate drinking
Green grass covered
Warm fire covers
Marshmallow warming
Hot food cooking
Steaming bath running.

Millie Wigington (8)
Sherwell Valley Primary School, Torquay

Ellie

There once was a girl called Ellie,
Whose legs were made out of jelly,
She saw Mr Hughes
And went on the news,
Who presented her with a wellie.

Nandaja Narayanan (8)
Sherwell Valley Primary School, Torquay

Firework Poem

Up
in
the
sky
boom!
Up
in
the
sky
crash!
Up
in
the
sky
scream!
The
crowd
roar
and
applaud.

Chloe Ratcliffe (7)
Sherwell Valley Primary School, Torquay

Old Man Jake

There was an old man called Jake,
Who dreamed of eating his cake,
He awoke with a fright
In the middle of the night
And found out he needed to bake.

Rebecca Roots (8)
Sherwell Valley Primary School, Torquay

There Was An Old Man

There was an old man called Dan
Who went to get a pan
To fry some pork
He used his fork
But still couldn't open a can.

Maisie Tysall (7)
Sherwell Valley Primary School, Torquay

Lou Trying To Go To the Loo

There was an old man called Lou
Who dreamed of eating a shoe.
He went to bed
And broke his head
And couldn't get up for a poo!

Haydon Green (8)
Sherwell Valley Primary School, Torquay

Nan's Rice Pudding

There once was a man called Dan,
Who dreamt of eating his nan.
He sprayed her with rice
To make her taste nice,
Then ate her up in a pan.

Owen Dawe-Smith (8)
Sherwell Valley Primary School, Torquay

In The Snow

The bare trees are swaying as fast as the wind.
The log cabin is covered in snow.
The stars in the sky are true diamonds,
The snowflakes twinkling like jewels.
The glowing mountains are moon silver,
The firewood outside the cabin won't be used now.
Look! Kids are coming to play,
The snow fall's a dream!

Lily James (8)
Sherwell Valley Primary School, Torquay

A Man Who Fell Off A Deck

There was an old man called Dan,
Who dreamt of eating a pan.
He broke his neck
And fell off the deck
Then fell on top of a van.

Jazmin Sherlock (8)
Sherwell Valley Primary School, Torquay

When I Went To The Zoo

When I went to the zoo,
An animal ate my shoe.
The gorilla ate my hat,
The tiger took my shirt,
The parrot chewed my socks.

At the zoo I ended up being Jungle Man.
At the zoo, I did, it's true.
Do you believe me?

Indie-May Taylor (8)
Sherwell Valley Primary School, Torquay

Clowns

Clowns, clowns, messing around,
Don't stop messing around.
Juggle the balls,
Throw the pies,
Honk the horn.
Now it's the end,
They say 'Farewell my friends'.

Kai Draper (8)
Sherwell Valley Primary School, Torquay

The Day I Went To Africa

The day I went to Africa
The giraffes played checkers.
The monkeys were wreckers,
The cheetahs were cheaters,
The lions needed heaters,
The leopards played with rocks,
The flamingo played near docks.
That was the day I went to Africa,
But the day I went to Florida,
Ahh!

Molly Hughes (8)
Sherwell Valley Primary School, Torquay

Food And Drinks

Monday I had nothing.
Tuesday I had a muffin.
Wednesday I had a glass of water.
Thursday I had a roast dinner.
Friday I had a glass of orange juice.
Saturday I had chocolate.
Sunday I had more!

Maxwell Pike (8)
Sherwell Valley Primary School, Torquay

Wouldn't It Be Funny

Wouldn't it be funny if your house could walk
And your eyes were made of rubber?
Wouldn't it be funny if we could fly,
Soaring up into the sky?
Wouldn't it be funny if we had two heads
And the insects and the plants played games?

Wouldn't it be funny?
It would be very funny indeed!

Ryan Owen (7)
Sherwell Valley Primary School, Torquay

Fireworks

F ireworks spin around
I eat hot dogs all the time
R oar in the sky
E ating sweets, I watch them
W ork their way up into the sky
O ver they go, over the moon and stars, and also houses
R ockets in the sky zooming
K aboom! Catherine wheels spinning round and round me.
   Making me dizzy.

Jess Goss (7)
Sherwell Valley Primary School, Torquay

Forests

In the forest were trees all around me.
The sun shone through the trees.
The leaves fell down on me.
It was so sunny, I couldn't look up.

Eloise Jackson (8)
Sherwell Valley Primary School, Torquay

Suck, Slurp, Down The Drain

Suck, slurp, down the drain,
Come on, come on, now use your brain.
Sucky, slurpy, plop,
The knickers go flop.
This all goes up in one big flame.
Flip-flop, the pencils go bop.
Flippy, floppy, the fish go pop.
It's always such woom!
Sometimes things go boom.
'Oh I'm sorry', as the beans go mopping!

Jacob Hogan (8)
Sherwell Valley Primary School, Torquay

Noisy Kitchen

The jelly on the plate went *boom!*
The spoon danced around in the kitchen!
The bowl rumbled and spun!
Then the eggs crashed onto the floor!
The fire in the stove went on!
Then the washer went *clang!* while it washed,
Then the cooker went on, it rumbled loudly!
Then the pans whacked each other hard!
Noisy!

Chase Ahearne (7)
Sherwell Valley Primary School, Torquay

The Bedroom

The bed goes *ping!*
And the curtains go *whoosh!*
The windows go *bang!*
And the doors go *slam!*
So that's what happens in the noisy bedroom.

Rachel Jones & Leah Gardner (8)
Sherwell Valley Primary School, Torquay

Fireworks

F ireworks crackle like stars in the sky.
I eat hot dogs, whilst the fire burns in the moonlight.
R ockets shoot up in the dark of night,
E ven dogs are trying to hide from the hot, orange, crackling fire.
W atching the rainbow-coloured fireworks,
    shouting up at the dark sky.
O n the darkest night fireworks crackle and pop in the sky.
R emoving the barbecue and the hot dogs go,
K icking the stones out of the way.
S tars flutter in the dark night,
    I think the dog had a fright.

Megan King (7)
Sherwell Valley Primary School, Torquay

The Crashing Sports Cars

Vroom, go the zooming sports cars
That whizz through the huge track
At 1,000 miles an hour
Mmmm, go the huge engines
Like millions of electric guitars
Playing in one small building

Zoooomm, go the cars
The cars leave fuel on the solid track
The thick huge cars roar
Across the huge, icy track.

Ryan Storey-Day (7), Harry Jamieson & Luke Lewis (8)
Sherwell Valley Primary School, Torquay

Horses, Ponies, Shires, Shetlands And Foals

Horses, ponies, Shires, Shetlands and foals,
They are all *beautifully* soft,
In the shadow of the willow tree
And up in the hayloft.

Horses, ponies, Shires, Shetlands and foals,
Fifty in the field,
Twenty horses stabled,
Thirty horses having a meal.

Horses, ponies, Shires, Shetlands and foals,
Loads of chestnuts,
Many of them stallions,
A couple of things said like, 'Tut, tut.'

Horses, ponies, Shires, Shetlands and foals,
Most of them on the moor,
Four of them up at the quarry,
Nine of them by Pew Tor.

Horses, ponies, Shires, Shetlands and foals,
A couple of them under a field tree,
The stable manager walked to the gate,
Buzzing around the head of Shire there was a bee.

Horses, ponies, Shires, Shetlands and foals,
The Shetlands are eating their food,
In the field,
While far away, someone is thinking about the creeds.

Horses, ponies, Shires, Shetlands and foals,
Half of them dappled greys,
The ostler caught one for grooming,
The other half are bays.

Miella Hayles (8)
Stuart Road Primary School, Plymouth

Mum And Dad

My mum and dad,
Are really fun,
Always and all of the time,
When we go camping in the sun.

My mum and dad,
We do what we like,
When we go to Central Park
We always take my bike.

My mum and dad,
Are really clever,
My mum got me my dog Lenny,
He's with me forever.

My mum and dad,
They are really kind,
My dad loves to swim,
He likes to swim with the tide.

Tia Woolcock (9)
Stuart Road Primary School, Plymouth

There's A Monkey At The Table

There's a monkey at the table
We all know that
So duck your head
I heard one of them spat

There's a monkey at the table
Run for your life
They're burping and fluffing
Don't forget your wife

There's a monkey at the table
As smelly as a rubbish pile
So I wouldn't come in happy
You won't go out with a smile

There's a monkey at the table
That's spitting food
There's a monkey at the table
They're in a bad mood.

James Braidford (8)
Stuart Road Primary School, Plymouth

Whales And Dolphins

We are creatures as flexible as can be
As quick as lightning
Less like a tree
We are friendly and hardly frightening.

We are peaceful creatures, as friendly as can be
We like to glide
And glisten in the sun
And swim with the tide.

We glide with pride
We are big and small
We jump as if we're flying
We are short and tall.

We sing as we jump
We're pointy and fat
We're more like athletes
And we can jump as high as a cat.

Jake Donkin-Peters (9)
Stuart Road Primary School, Plymouth

Midnight Feat

In the moonlit night, me and my brother are wide awake,
Just like an owl.
I sneak into my brother's room and knock,
We decide to have a feast.

We creep to the kitchen,
As quiet as mice,
We climb on the work surface,
See what is in the top cupboard.

I tiptoe round the gloomy corridors
To get a blanket.
I creep back, the floor is ice-cold
And me and my brother eat the midnight feast.

Tara Waterfield (8)
Stuart Road Primary School, Plymouth

My Lawn Mower

It can be found in an old, smelly garden shed,
It is a man who is trying to suck you up
When you are lying on the peaceful grass.
It whips up the grass into its blades in about two seconds.
It reminds me of a monster, eating all the grass
Into its greedy, eating tummy.

Abby Fletcher (9)
The Clinton CE Primary School, Merton

Sunshine

S hining down,
U pon the Earth,
N urturing plants,
S himmering down, the plants start dying,
H earing the birds calling above the colourful plants,
I ntensive sun,
N earby the plants withering away,
E nd of life for all the beautiful daffodils and dandelions.

Chelsey Weeks (9)
The Clinton CE Primary School, Merton

Ye Old Axe

A killer blade, ready to chop up its prey
An unexpected surprise, as it hunts down the unexpected
A guard dog, waiting to chew up a robber's head
It's bad, it's mean, it's very keen
As shiny silver as a car wheel, getting muddy every second
Chop, chop, chop, goes ye old axe
Dangerous to touch as it would take your fingers off!

Annabel Halstead (9)
The Clinton CE Primary School, Merton

The Garden Fork

She has devil's teeth, sharp and pointy,
Her face is scratched.
She lives in a garden shed,
At the bottom of the garden.
The shed is cold and draughty.
She hopes she'll be pulled for work soon,
Because the shed is draughty.
Her tongue is ruby-red
And is as long as a garden hose,
Her friends don't like playing with her,
Because she is mean and nips them hard.
She is the smallest in her family,
Her family is kind and loving,
Her friends like her family, not like the rest!
See you tomorrow little one,
We'll leave you now to dream,
Another one of your friends will come
And stay with you.

Charlotte Swain (9)
The Clinton CE Primary School, Merton

Watering Can

An elephant squirting out water from its trunk.
A rhino with fresh, new tusks.
Drip, drip, drip!

A kettle filling a giant cup.
A shower spitting out water.
Drip, drip drip!

An elephant sucking up water from the lake.
Drip, drip, drip!

Chris Ashton (10)
The Clinton CE Primary School, Merton

The Garden Gloves

A pair of hands, wriggling, with fingers,
scuttling across the weed-grown path,
like a weed grown forest,
growing wild along by the green hillside verge.

Granny slips the gloves over her needle-like fingers,
starts digging silently in the rose bed,
to take out the old, ready for new.

The skin of the gloves feels like a nasty, horrible warthog,
that has rolled in something revolting.

Hungry, in from the cold, fish fingers waiting for my tea,
reminds me of the orange-fingered garden gloves.

A pot of pens grouped together like garden canes,
always smells like rotting runner beans
that have grown up from the earth.

Danielle Payne (10)
The Clinton CE Primary School, Merton

The Magical Gloves

Hiding under the cobwebs in the dirty garden shed.
Creeping out of the dirty garden shed.
Waiting to explore the garden.
I help pull the weeds,
Preparing the ground, ready for planting.
Like a pair of rats, scuttles around the garden.
As dogs, digging out their bones, from piles of leaves.
Like children waiting for their play,
Waiting to be washed after a long summer's day.

Hannah Loufer (11)
The Clinton CE Primary School, Merton

The Garden Monster

It's crooked, rusty and a monster
As tall and ghostly as the spooky bear haunted trees
Scoop, ouch, scoop!

Scaring all the night creatures away
A master to all night creatures
Enemy to garden residents
Scoop, ouch, scoop!

No creature would dare eat the yummy bug
On the razor-sharp blade
Any bug would be killed by the spiteful blades
Scoop, ouch, scoop!

Mashing up any creature in its path
Leaving a horrid slimy trail behind it
Killing the strongest of grass
Scoop, ouch, scoop!

Offending every bug that ventured into the garden
Killing every plant
Scoop, ouch, scoop!

Pip Mahoney (9)
The Clinton CE Primary School, Merton

Hosepipe

Hosepipes can be lots of fun,
My mummy always says.
Having fun with water, playing with friends.
Water squirting out the end.
My friends all end up soaking wet,
It sprays out like an elephant's jet.
Hosepipe water, lots of fun,
Let's start all over again.

Thomas Wright (9)
The Clinton CE Primary School, Merton

Hosepipes

Lying in a bundle, left all day, pouring down.
It's a colossal piece of string, trying to escape from my drawer.
A wriggly piece of spaghetti, holding onto my plate.
Drip! Drop! Drip!

It's a lonely earthworm, running away from home,
digging deeper underground.
A tiny piece of seaweed, holding onto another one,
hiding in a coral reef from a hungry scuba-diver.
It's a slimy snail trail, leading to a hidden garden
that no one knows about.
An endless rope that no one knows where it's leading to, except for it
goes through a prickly hedge.
Splish! Splash! Splish!

It's a piece of hair, climbing on your head,
disturbing all the other hairs.
A bit of ice, floating on a small pond,
watching little fish swim to school.
It's a bright, green pen, ready to be used once again for another day.
A bunch of arms strangling me for my life.

Emily Hookway (10)
The Clinton CE Primary School, Merton

Hosepipe

It's a slimy snake, hiding in the garden.
An endless tube, circling round.
Drip! Drop! Drip!

A shiny cobra, spraying out its venom at his victim.
A necklace for a giant.
Squeeze! Squirt! Spray!

Wiggly worms, slithering away from the giant snake.
It sounds like a waterfall, falling from the rocks.
It's a dog sitting on my doorstep waiting to be fed.

Squirt!

Lydia Wade (10)
The Clinton CE Primary School, Merton

Hosepipe

It's a small piece of spaghetti, attached to your tap.
It's a haunted, green boa constrictor.
It's an endless tube, no one knows where the end is.

Inside it has powerful liquid, squashing its way out.
It's sitting at my door waiting to be fed.
It's a snake strangling a helpless, little child,
With all its power and strength.
It's spraying all his venom over his prey.
It sounds like a waterfall, falling down the rocks.
It smells like an old, rotten sock.
It feels all slippery and slimy
. . . our hosepipe!

Megan Chapman (9)
The Clinton CE Primary School, Merton

The Knight's Tale

The knight was in his castle, eating his dinner,
His armour was all shiny, he really was a winner.
He heard a fierce dragon at the castle door,
It really was so noisy it must be against the law.
That awful noise was so bad in my head,
He really was so angry, he was seeing red.
He grabbed his sword, his shield and his lance,
He'd chase it all the way to France.
But when the angry knight walked out the castle,
He was in for a big surprise.
He looked all around to find the dragon staring him in the eyes.
The dragon was a gentle beast and didn't want a scrap,
So they both sat down by the moat and had a nice long chat.

Aidan Wright (8)
The Clinton CE Primary School, Merton

Sunset

S un shining down
U nderneath the clouds
N ever the same
S etting in the sky
E vening of colour
T ill it gets dark.

Lauren Butler (11)
The Clinton CE Primary School, Merton

The Pied Piper

The town was full of rats,
Rats as big as a pussy cat,
In the German market store,
The piper arrived,
Blew his pipe
The rats drowned in the river.

The mayor didn't pay,
So the piper slew the children,
The people of the town slew the mayor.

Greg Bolam-Green (10)
Thorner's CE Primary School, Dorchester

My Dog

My dog is as black as night,
With snowy paws and eyes so bright.
She's a stuffy pig, she eats so much,
At least she doesn't sniff my crotch!
She used to leap and bound like a rabbit,
But now she's old she's lost the habit.
When she gets home she is as stiff as a board,
But when she's on her bed she always snores!

Annie Nobes (9)
Thorner's CE Primary School, Dorchester

Doggy Wonder

Wet as a fish,
messy like a dish,
looks like a cow,
can't really miaow.

Stuck in the rain,
been called such a pain,
infested with fleas,
peeing on trees.

Cars flying by,
looks like a sty,
comes back to his bed,
quickly gets fed.

Aaron Sinclair (10)
Thorner's CE Primary School, Dorchester

Rosie

Rosie, the dog, has eyes like a tennis ball,
Her paws are like velvet gloves.
When she stands up her legs are so tall
And there is so much that she loves.

Her nose is like a cold, black stone,
Her teeth are pearly white,
She loves to chew on a meaty bone,
But she hates going out at night.

Rosie's tongue is long and pink,
She runs around the trunk of a tree,
Her tail swishes, she's as quick as a blink,
She stops and scratches at an annoying flea.

Imogen Slade (9)
Thorner's CE Primary School, Dorchester

The Collie

The Collie dog is a bundle of life and happiness,
At first, before it is trained,
It's like a baby, nappiless.

The Collie dog is the wind when it runs,
It just seems to absolutely fly,
It looks similar to lightning,
When it zigzags across the sky.

The Collie dog is a machine,
That makes us stay together,
It's always ready to round you up,
But most of all, and don't forget,
The Collie dog is your friend forever.

Flora Jevons (10)
Thorner's CE Primary School, Dorchester

Jason, The Alsatian

Jason, the Alsatian, has feet like ducks,
When you go for a walk he chases animals which cluck.
After the rain his fur really smells,
When my dad needs him, he always yells.

Jason's fur is as soft as rugs,
When you take him for a walk he always tugs.
His tail is a whip, which is just being swung,
He always picks up things that are flung.

Jason's tongue is long and cold,
He is only two, which is not very old.
His bark is as loud as a lion's *roar,*
When he has eaten his food, he begs for more.

Lucie Fry (9)
Thorner's CE Primary School, Dorchester

Me, The River

Shilly shally down the mountains
I gurgle to the top of fountains
Rotten abandoned boats, chained to my banks
Nearby appears life-wrecking poison tank
All my happiness and joy gone.

I have travelled down the ages
I have seen secret pages
But people still treat me like a rubbish tip.

Where have the children been?
Only crumbling houses have seen
I used to be full of children's laughs
But now it's just abandoned paths
All my happiness and joy gone.

Finally the countryside is here
The birds are singing near
On an old oak tree
I am rubbish free
All my happiness and joy are here.

Annabel Armstrong (10)
Thorner's CE Primary School, Dorchester

The Wet Dog

The wet dog shook all the water off
Like a leaf in a hailstorm
His paws that were bushy and ragged and joined by muddy leaves.
His mop joined to his back, which some people call a tail
Was dripping on the coal like floor, in the pitch-black night.

The thunder boomed like a huge Indian drum
But then lightning struck,
Like a knife through a pillow it crackled and cracked
Then the door opened, it was the door to the heavens
The dog darted into the house like a cheetah
He snuggled into his bed as a dog would
And squeezed his bones off to sleep for another day.

Harry Lockett
Thorner's CE Primary School, Dorchester

Swan On The Surface

I am a graceful white swan
Being pulled along the river,
I can see colourful fish
Darting in and out of the reeds below me.
The view is rushing past me.
As the current pulls me along,
Sometimes I see bubbles in front of me,
Bobbing up and down,
Then they pop as I touch them
With my feathered finger.

The river is crystal clear,
There is a rainbow
Appearing from the clouds.
I can see birds gliding
Across the sky.
One cloud is shaped like a playful kitten,
I had better watch out then.
See the reflection of the rainbow in the river.

I'm going to get out now
But I'll come back tomorrow.

Sarah Bird (10)
Thorner's CE Primary School, Dorchester

Doggies

Quick as a cheetah
Tricky as a flea
Cute as a bunny
When she licks me

A hairy mud ball
Appears out of a puddle
There's no way today
I'll give you a cuddle!

Dionne Sinclair (9)
Thorner's CE Primary School, Dorchester

Little Dog

Little dog, on his own
As hungry as can be
Lights make him lick his lips
Makes it feel like home.

Smells like sick
As he walks around
Getting wet every second
As he's walking on the ground.

Rachel Talbot (9)
Thorner's CE Primary School, Dorchester

My Dog, Bolo

My dog, Bolo, has teeth like a sharks
Ears like tigers eating jam tarts
His nose is the pink of an old cloth
When he sneezes it's like hurricanes lifting off
His mouth is like a crimson door opened
When he sleeps, don't walk past
Just try not to be the last
If you hear a bark
You'd better run like a spark.

Tarren Harlet Hogshaw (10)
Thorner's CE Primary School, Dorchester

River Snake

The river is a snake,
It's fast and dangerous
And will kill at first sight.
It squirms past the rocks
Like a wiggly worm.
It's venomous and has sharp, rocky teeth.

William Bowen-Ashwin (9)
Thorner's CE Primary School, Dorchester

Dexter

You may call his tum a tall church spire,
His tail looks like black and white fire,
His nose is a piece of dark, black coal,
No wonder, after digging a great big hole.

His soft, brown eyes, dark as deep pools,
At other times sparkle like jewels,
His ears are long and soft as silk,
His velvet coat is as white as milk.

He growls as loud as a rumbling train,
He often barks at the wind and rain,
His paws are big, like dinner plates,
Me and Dexter are best of mates.

Honor Slade (10)
Thorner's CE Primary School, Dorchester

The Streets

Out on the street
Nobody cares,
His body is a rainy cloud
In the sky.

At night you see
Bright, orange eyes,
But when you walk there
It's the shop lights.

People chuck litter down,
Streets looking like storms,
Drains full of water
Look like rivers running by.

Rebecca Talbot (10)
Thorner's CE Primary School, Dorchester

The Candle

The glimmering, the shimmering
White and orange flame
Flickers in the night-time
Over and over again.

The peaceful scent of lavender
Filling all the air,
Lighting up the empty room,
Sparkles everywhere.

Shadows on the ceiling,
Shadows on the floor,
Tiny sparks of orange light
Shining on the door.

Suddenly through the window
A gust of wind did come.
Emptiness fills the room,
The candle flame has gone.

Sitting in the blackness,
Smoky darkness all around,
The tiny fire has died away,
It left without a sound.

Lucy Everist (10)
Vinehall School, Robertsbridge

The Haunted House

Scary in the haunted house
Tiptoe quiet, like a mouse
Shadows flicker on the wall
Some are short and some are tall
Bats and spiders hide and creep
While the witches go to sleep
A book we find with spells and more
Then a creak comes from the door
Eyes peek through, we hear a spell
Nervous through my fear, I yell
Strangest thing I've ever seen
Turning slimy, going green!
I try to scream, but when I shout
'Ribbit,' is all that comes out
Can't think straight, don't know why
All a frog can do is sigh
With webbed feet I can't run fast
How long will this bad spell last?
Round the corner, through the gate
Jump over this, I escape my fate
The spell wears off and now you see
Sweet, tall, pretty me.

Gemma Robinson (10)
Vinehall School, Robertsbridge

School Lunch

Do you want to know the truth about what's inside school lunch?
Well here you go, ingredients, but it's a disgusting bunch.

For soup: get some spiders, worms and a slug or two,
Add some stock, boil till a sickly blue
And there are definitely no croutons here,
(it's actually brains dipped in beer).

The main course is dead frog pie,
Horrid enough to make you cry.
Get dog's droppings and cow pat, mixed nice and thick,
Bake well and give a stir and add a spoon of sick.
Next, get a dozen frogs (make sure they're dead)
Then stir with blood so it's bright red.
Mix both together with water, straight from the loo,
Make sure a browny-green and don't forget to stew.

For pudding it's revolting jelly,
I'm sure it comes from a cow's belly
And instead of chocolate shavings, we get bits of chrome.
So here's some advice, next time bring lunch from home!

Kajal Radia (10)
Vinehall School, Robertsbridge

Chocolate

Chocolate is sweet,
It's a really big treat,
It's yummy and creamy,
Ooh, just *so* dreamy,
And people say it's *bad* for you!

Bad . . . how can it be bad?
It can make you happy when you are sad,
It makes you smile through your tears,
And I loved for just *so* many years!
And people say it's *bad* for you!

Dark chocolate is really scrummy,
I eat a lot, just ask my mummy!
It is not just fantastically delicious,
It is also really, *very* nutritious,
And people say it's *bad* for you!

Have a chunk, a good old piece,
And don't get caught by the chocolate police,
Now you know it's good for you,
Every word I have written is true,
Don't listen to people who say it's bad for you!

Saffia Dalton (9)
Vinehall School, Robertsbridge

Dangers Of The Deep

The dangers of the Deep,
Giant squid and octopus
And those jagged rocks beneath,
Also the unfriendly sharks will
Bite you with their teeth.

The dangers of the Deep,
Swim away from the rogue currents,
Catch a ride on whale, who knows,
It could flip you off
With its huge, blue wrinkly tail.

The dangers of the Deep,
You shouldn't be scared of glowing eels
Until you've seen an
Angry, charging, powerful seal,
And I'll tell you something, you could be its meal.

The dangers of the Deep,
At the end of this journey
If you're a diver,
You'll be battered and bruised,
If you're a survivor.

Ursula Horton (9)
Vinehall School, Robertsbridge

The Perfect English Garden

The perfect English garden
Is not what you might see,
At a perfect English manor house,
Through acres of shrubs there might be.

The perfect English garden
Is often found at home,
Where birds can rest and recoup
And wild animals are free to roam.

The perfect English garden
Is never neat and prim,
With twigs and leaves all over the place
And hedges needing a trim.

The perfect English garden
Has ivy, allowed to grow
Up walls and trees and everywhere
And grass that needs a mow.

The perfect English garden
Has masses of trees galore,
Oaks and pines and birches,
With chestnut and sycamores.

The perfect English garden
Is where pretty roses settle,
But is treated the same
As the ugly common nettle.

The perfect English garden
Always has to be,
Where you'll find happiness
And peace and sanctuary.

Isabelle Powell (11)
Vinehall School, Robertsbridge

The Sea

As the sea cradles a ship, gently, in its strong, firm arms,
Waves ripple and splash as the wind commands.
With the gentle glow of sun, such an enchanted, magical touch,
The water ripples discreetly with a sprinkle of rays, not much,
Are dancing with the water, wind and the waves.

As the light dims, a rumble is heard,
At once the water is distilled and disturbed.
The sea roars and at a fearsome touch
The ship is twisted and toppled as such.

With wind as its master, the sea crushes the boat
And sends out a cry on an anguished note.

The sea's work is overlooked,
Another day begins,
The shrill note still rings,
But the sound does not reach our ears,
For this is the sound of the waves bitter-sweet tears.

Chloë Jeremy (11)
Vinehall School, Robertsbridge

Winter

Icy streets, frosty grass,
Winter's coming very fast.
The flowers are gone, they never stay,
But they will grow back in May.
The bonfire is finally lit,
Everyone watches and sits.
The birds are flying away,
They will return on a warmer day.
Everyone's tucked up in their bed, nice and tight,
The days are getting darker, not much light.
The fire is burning, so warm, so hot,
All the Christmas cooking is done in a big pot.
Snowball fights in the street,
What a lovely winter treat.

Aneesa Zaidi (10)
Vinehall School, Robertsbridge

Country Poems

In Greece there are police,
Who have smelly feet,
While pounding the beat.

In New York they always eat pork,
With a spoon and fork,
Before taking a walk.

In Scotland they wear kilts
And run around on stilts,
While drinking milk.

In Wales rugby is played,
Before getting a maid,
Then they sit in the shade.

Josh Ball (9)
Woolacombe School, Woolacombe

Nonsense Places

In Antigua
Amena
Drinks Ribena.

In Bombay
The people say
It's raining every day.

In San Francisco
They eat in the bistro,
Then go to the disco.

In Peru
They go to the zoo
And say toodleoo.

Amena Mordin (8)
Woolacombe School, Woolacombe

Alphabet Of Horrendously Horrible Habits

A is for Alex, who walks on his toes,
B is for Bernard, who picks his nose.
C is for Connor, who never washes his hands,
D is for Dennis, who flicks elastic bands.
E is for Emma, who likes robbing banks,
F is for Frank, who likes to play pranks.
G is for Georgie, who always wears dresses,
H is for Halli, who always makes messes.
I is for Isabel, who always eats jelly,
J is for Jacob, who has a big belly.
K is for Katie, who is always late,
L is for Lolly, who licks her plate.
M is for Morgan, who never says please,
N is for Nelly, who loves peas.
O is for Olli, who hates dollies,
P is for Penny, who always eats lollies.
Q is for Quebert, who plays with girls,
R is for Ronny who has lots of curls.
S is for Sally, who always has a plait,
T is for Tom, who keeps a rat.
U is for Uncle, who talks to the wall,
V is for Verity, who is very tall.
W is for William, who likes to surf,
X is for Xavier, who lives on a turf.
Y is for Yasmine, who likes to plant plants,
Z is for Zac, who never wears pants.

Eliza King-Smith (8)
Woolacombe School, Woolacombe

Alphabet Characters

A is for Andrew who likes to chatter,
B is for Billy, who thinks it doesn't matter.
C is for Colin, who likes to bully,
D is for Dave who always wears a woolly.
E is for Eliot, who likes to pick and flick,
F is for Frankenstein who always has to pick.
G is for Gertrude, who always answers back,
H if for Henry who always carries a sack.
I is for Ivy, who loves to do pranks,
J is for Jamie, who never wears pants.
K is for Kate who always plays with nukes,
L is for Luke, who always likes to puke.
M is for Matthew, who always has to play,
N is for Nigel, who has decay.
O is for Oscar, who is a real pain,
P is for Pam, who loves to play in the rain.
Q is for Queen, who loves to boast,
R is for Ryan who loves to push people off the boat.
S is for Steve, who loves to stay up late,
T is for Timmy, who never eats off a plate.
U is for Usif, who loves to dance.
V is for Victor, who lives in France.
W is for William, who always hurts,
X is for Xavier, who always wears shirts.
Y is for Yarik, who likes to poke,
Z is for Zachary, who sometimes likes to choke.

Matthew Porter (8)
Woolacombe School, Woolacombe

Spider

In the spider there is an eye,
In the eye there is a web,
In the web there is blood,
In the blood there is poison.
In the poison there is death,
In the death there is fear,
In the fear there is a spider,

Connor O'Toole (8)
Woolacombe School, Woolacombe

Elephant's Ears

In an elephant's ear a desert is boiling.
The trunk of an elephant is constantly coiling.
The mouth of an elephant is yanking and hoisting.
In the desert the elephant's boiling.

Liam Lynas (9)
Woolacombe School, Woolacombe

Under The . . .

Under the tiger's paw is his camouflaged lair,
Under the lair an adder's fang poisons a small eagle.
Under the eagle's heart is the hope of his chicks,
Under the chick's beak is the poacher's desire,
In the poacher's heart is the tiger from the past.

Jack Denzey Draper (9)
Woolacombe School, Woolacombe

Young Writers Information

We hope you have enjoyed reading this book - and that you will continue to enjoy it in the coming years.

If you like reading and writing poetry drop us a line, or give us a call, and we'll send you a free information pack.

Alternatively if you would like to order further copies of this book or any of our other titles, then please give us a call or log onto our website at www.youngwriters.co.uk

**Young Writers Information
Remus House
Coltsfoot Drive
Peterborough
PE2 9JX**

(01733) 890066